Kitchener's Mob

James Norman Hall

Contents

THE PREAMBLE.	34
LAWS by Plato	215
BOOK I.	215
BOOK II.	242
BOOK III.	265
BOOK IV.	293
BOOK V.	313
BOOK VI.	332
BOOK VII.	364
BOOK VIII.	401
BOOK IX.	423
BOOK X.	452
BOOK XI.	480
BOOK XII.	505

KITCHENER'S MOB

BY

James Norman Hall

TO
TOMMY
OF THE GREAT WAR
WHO IS ADDING IMMORTAL LUSTER
TO THE NAME OF
ATKINS

Note

This brief narrative is by no means a complete record of life in a battalion of one of Lord Kitchener's first armies. It is, rather, a story in outline, a mere suggestion of that life as it is lived in the British lines along the western front. If those who read gain thereby a more intimate view of trench warfare, and of the men who are so gallantly and cheerfully laying down their lives for England, the purpose of the writer will have been accomplished.

The diagram which appears on the front and rear covers of the book is a partially conventionalized design illustrating some features of trench construction mentioned in Chapter VI. For obvious reasons it is not drawn to scale, and although it is a truthful representation of a typical segment of the British line, it is not an exact sketch of any existing sector.

April, 1916.

CHAPTER I
JOINING UP

"Kitchener's Mob" they were called in the early days of August, 1914, when London hoardings were clamorous with the first calls for volunteers. The seasoned regulars of the first British expeditionary force said it patronizingly, the great British public hopefully, the world at large doubtfully. "Kitchener's Mob," when there was but a scant sixty thousand under arms with millions yet to come. "Kitchener's Mob" it remains to-day, fighting in hundreds of thousands in France, Belgium, Africa, the Balkans. And to-morrow, when the war is ended, who will come marching home again, old campaigners, war-worn remnants of once mighty armies? "Kitchener's Mob."

It is not a pleasing name for the greatest volunteer army in the history of the world; for more than three millions of toughened, disciplined fighting men, united under one flag, all parts of one magnificent military organization. And yet Kitchener's own Tommies are responsible for it, the rank and file, with their inherent love of ridicule even at their own expense, and their intense dislike of "swank." They fastened the name upon themselves, lest the world at large should think they regarded themselves too highly. There it hangs. There it will hang for all time.

It was on the 18th of August, 1914, that the mob spirit gained its mastery over me. After three weeks of solitary tramping in the mountains of North Wales, I walked suddenly into news of the great war, and went at once to London, with a longing for home which seemed strong enough to carry me through the week of idleness until my boat should sail. But, in a spirit of adventure, I suppose, I tempted myself with the possibility of assuming the increasingly popular alias, Atkins. On two successive mornings I joined the long line of prospective recruits before the offices at Great Scotland Yard, withdrawing each time, after moving a convenient distance toward the desk of the recruiting sergeant. Disregarding the proven fatality of third times, I joined it on another morning, dangerously near to the head of the procession.

"Now, then, you! Step along!"

There is something compelling about a military command, given by a military officer accustomed to being obeyed. While the doctors were thumping me, measuring me, and making an inventory of "physical peculiarities, if any," I tried to analyze my unhesitating, almost instinctive reaction to that stern, confident "Step along!" Was it an act of weakness, a want of character, evidenced by my inability to say no? Or was it the blood of military forebears asserting itself after many years of inanition? The latter conclusion being the more pleasing, I decided that I was the grandson of my Civil War grandfather, and the worthy descendant of stalwart warriors of a yet earlier period.

I was frank with the recruiting officers. I admitted, rather boasted, of my American citizenship, but expressed my entire willingness to serve in the British army in case this should not expatriate me. I had, in fact, delayed, hoping that an American legion would be formed in London as had been done in Paris. The announcement was received with some surprise. A brief conference was held, during which there was much vigorous shaking of heads. While I awaited the decision I thought of the steamship ticket in my pocket. I remembered that my boat was to sail on Friday. I thought of my plans for the future and anticipated the joy of an early home-coming. Set against this was the prospect of an indefinite period of soldiering among strangers. "Three years or the duration of the war" were the terms of the enlistment contract. I had visions of bloody engagements, of feverish nights in hospital, of endless years in a home for disabled soldiers. The conference was over, and the recruiting officer returned to his desk, smiling broadly.

"We'll take you, my lad, if you want to join. You'll just say you are an Englishman, won't you, as a matter of formality?" Here was an avenue of escape, beckoning me like an alluring country road winding over the hills of home. I refused it with the same instinctive swiftness of decision that had brought me to the medical inspection room. And a few moments later, I took "the King's shilling," and promised, upon my oath as a loyal British subject, to bear true allegiance to the Union Jack.

During the completion of other, less important formalities, I was taken in charge by a sergeant who might have stepped out of any of the "Barrack-Room Ballads." He was true to type to the last twist in the s of Atkins. He told me of service in India, Egypt, South Africa. He showed me both scars and medals with that air of "Now-I-would-n't-do-this-for-any-one-but-you" which is so flattering to the novice. He gave me advice as to my best method of procedure when I should go to Hounslow Barracks to join my unit.

"'An 'ere! Wotever you do an' wotever you s'y, don't forget to myke the lads think you're an out-an'-outer, if you understand my meaning,--a Britisher, you know. They'll tyke to you. Strike me blind! Be free an' easy with 'em,--no swank, mind you!--an' they'll be downright pals with you. You're different, you know. But don't put on no airs. Wot I mean is, don't let 'em think that you think you're different. See wot I mean?"

I said that I did.

"An' another thing; talk like 'em."

I confessed that this might prove to be rather a large contract.

"'Ard? S'y! 'Ere! If I 'ad you fer a d'y, I'd 'ave you talkin' like a born Lunnoner! All you got to do is forget all them aitches. An' you don't want to s'y 'can't,' like that. S'y 'cawrn't.'"

I said it.

"Now s'y, 'Gor blimy, 'Arry, 'ow's the missus?'"

I did.

"That's right! Oh, you'll soon get the swing of it."

There was much more instruction of the same nature. By the time I was ready to leave the recruiting offices I felt that I had made great progress in the vernacular. I said good-bye to the sergeant warmly. As I was about to leave he made the most peculiar and amusing gesture of a man drinking.

"A pint o' mild an' bitter," he said confidentially. "The boys always gives me the price of a pint."

"Right you are, sergeant!" I used the expression like a born Englishman. And with the liberality of a true soldier, I gave him my shilling, my first day's wage as a British fighting man.

The remainder of the week I spent mingling with the crowds of enlisted men at the Horse Guards Parade, watching the bulletin boards for the appearance of my name which would mean that I was to report at the regimental depot at Hounslow. My first impression of the men with whom I was to live for three years, or the duration of the war, was anything but favorable. The newspapers had been asserting that the new army was being recruited from the flower of England's young manhood. The throng at the Horse Guards Parade resembled an army of the unemployed, and I thought it likely that most of them were misfits, out-of-works, the kind of men who join the army because they can do nothing else. There were, in fact, a good many of these. I soon learned, however, that the general out-at-elbows appearance was due to another cause. A genial Cockney gave me the hint.

"'Ave you joined up, matey?" he asked.

I told him that I had.

"Well, 'ere's a friendly tip for you. Don't wear them good clo'es w'en you goes to the depot. You won't see 'em again likely, an' if you gets through the war you might be a-wantin' of 'em. Wear the worst rags you got."

I profited by the advice, and when I fell in, with the other recruits for the Royal Fusiliers, I felt much more at my ease.

CHAPTER II
ROOKIES

A mob" is genuinely descriptive of the array of would-be soldiers which crowded the long parade-ground at Hounslow Barracks during that memorable last week in August. We herded together like so many sheep. We had lost our individuality, and it was to be months before we regained it in a new aspect, a collective individuality of which we became increasingly proud. We squeak-squawked across the barrack square in boots which felt large enough for an entire family of feet. Our khaki service dress uniforms were strange and uncomfortable. Our hands hung limply along the seams of our pocketless trousers. Having no place in which to conceal them, and nothing for them to do, we tried to ignore them. Many a Tommy, in a moment of forgetfulness, would make a dive for the friendly pockets which were no longer there. The look of sheepish disappointment, as his hands slid limply down his trouser-legs, was most comical to see. Before many days we learned the uses to which soldiers' hands are put. But for the moment they seemed absurdly unnecessary.

We must have been unpromising material from the military point of view. That was evidently the opinion of my own platoon sergeant. I remember, word for word, his address of welcome, one of soldier-like brevity and pointedness, delivered while we stood awkwardly at attention on the barrack square.

"Lissen 'ere, you men! I've never saw such a raw, roun'-shouldered batch o' rookies in fifteen years' service. Yer pasty-faced an' yer thin-chested. Gawd 'elp 'Is Majesty if it ever lays with you to save 'im! 'Owever, we're 'ere to do wot we can with wot we got. Now, then, upon the command, 'Form Fours,' I wanna see the even numbers tyke a pace to the rear with the left foot, an' one to the right with the right foot. Like so: 'One-one-two!' Platoon! Form Fours! Oh! Orful! Orful! As y' were! As y' were!"

If there was doubt in the minds of any of us as to our rawness, it was quickly dispelled by our platoon sergeants, regulars of long standing, who had been left in England to assist in whipping the new armies into shape. Naturally, they were disgruntled at this, and we offered them such splendid opportunities for working off overcharges of spleen. We had come to Hounslow, believing that, within a few weeks' time, we should be fighting in France, side by side with the men of the first British expeditionary force. Lord Kitchener had said that six months of training, at the least, was essential. This statement we regarded as intentionally misleading. Lord Kitchener was too shrewd a soldier to announce his plans; but England needed men badly, immediately. After a week of training, we should be proficient in the use of our rifles. In addition to this, all that was needed was the ability to form fours and march, in column of route, to the station where we should entrain for Folkestone or Southampton, and France.

As soon as the battalion was up to strength, we were given a day of preliminary drill before proceeding to our future training area in Essex. It was a disillusioning experience. Equally disappointing was the undignified display of our little skill, at Charing Cross Station, where we performed before a large and amused London audience. For my own part, I could scarcely wait until we were safely hidden within the train. During the journey to Colchester, a re-enlisted Boer War veteran, from the inaccessible heights of South African experience, enfiladed us with a fire of sarcastic comment.

"I'm a-go'n' to transfer out o' this 'ere mob, that's wot I'm a go'n' to do! Soldiers! S'y! I'll bet a quid they ain't a one of you ever saw a rifle before! Soldiers? Strike me pink! Wot's Lord Kitchener a-doin' of, that's wot I want to know!"

The rest of us smoked in wrathful silence, until one of the boys demonstrated to the Boer War veteran that he knew, at least, how to use his fists. There was some bloodshed, followed by reluctant apologies on the part of the Boer warrior. It was one of innumerable differences of opinion which I witnessed during the months that followed. And most of them were settled in the same decisive way.

Although mine was a London regiment, we had men in the ranks from all parts of the United Kingdom. There were North-Countrymen, a few Welsh, Scotch, and Irish, men from the Midlands and from the south of England. But for the most part we were Cockneys, born within the sound of Bow Bells. I had planned to follow the friendly advice of the recruiting sergeant. "Talk like 'em," he had said. Therefore, I struggled bravely with the peculiarities of the Cockney twang, recklessly dropped aitches when I should have kept them, and prefixed them indiscriminately before every convenient aspirate. But all my efforts were useless. The imposition was apparent to my fellow Tommies immediately. I had only to begin speaking, within the hearing of a genuine Cockney, when he would say, "'Ello! w'ere do you come from? The Stites?" or, "I'll bet a tanner you're a Yank!" I decided to make a confession, and I have been glad, ever since, that I did. The boys gave me a warm and hearty welcome when they learned that I was a sure-enough American. They called me "Jamie the Yank." I was a piece of tangible evidence of the bond of sympathy existing between the two great English-speaking nations. I told them of the many Americans of German extraction, whose sympathies were honestly and sincerely on the other side. But they would not have it so. I was the personal representative of the American people. My presence in the British army was proof positive of this.

Being an American, it was very hard, at first, to understand the class distinctions of British army life. And having understood them, it was more difficult yet to endure them. I learned that a ranker, or private soldier, is a socially inferior being from the officer's point of view. The officer class and the ranker class are east and west, and never the twain shall meet, except in their respective places upon the parade-ground. This does not hold good, to the same extent, upon active service. Hardships and dangers, shared in common, tend to break down artificial barriers. But even then, although there was good-will and friendliness between officers and men, I saw nothing of genuine comradeship. This seemed to me a great pity. It was a loss for the officers fully as much as it was for the men.

I had to accept, for convenience sake, the fact of my social inferiority. Centuries of army tradition demanded it; and I discovered that it is absolutely futile for one inconsequential American to rebel against the unshakable fortress of English tradition. Nearly all of my comrades were used to clear-cut class distinctions in civilian life. It made little difference to them that some of our officers were recruits as raw as were we ourselves. They had money enough and education enough and influence enough to secure the king's commission; and that fact was proof enough for Tommy that they were gentlemen, and, therefore, too good for the likes of him to be associating with.

"Look 'ere! Ain't a gentleman a gentleman? I'm arskin' you, ain't 'e?"

I saw the futility of discussing this question with Tommy. And later, I realized how important for British army discipline such distinctions are.

So great is the force of prevailing opinion that I sometimes found myself accepting Tommy's point of view. I wondered if I was, for some eugenic reason, the inferior of these men whom I had to "Sir" and salute whenever I dared speak. Such lapses were only occasional. But I understood, for the first time, how important a part circumstance and environment play in shaping one's mental attitude. How I longed, at times, to chat with colonels and to joke with captains on terms of equality! Whenever I confided these aspirations to Tommy he gazed at me in awe.

"Don't be a bloomin' ijut! They could jolly well 'ang you fer that!"

CHAPTER III
THE MOB IN TRAINING

The Nth Service Battalion, Royal Fusiliers, on the march was a sight not easily to be forgotten. To the inhabitants of Colchester, Folkestone, Shorncliffe, Aldershot, and other towns and villages throughout the south of England, we were well known. We displayed ourselves with what must have seemed to them a shameless disregard for appearances. Our approach was announced by a discordant tumult of fifes and drums, for our band, of which later, we became justly proud, was a newly fledged and still imperfect organization. Windows were flung up and doors thrown open along our line of march; but alas, we were greeted with no welcome glances of kindly approval, no waving of handkerchiefs, no clapping of hands. Nursemaids, who are said to have a nice and discriminating eye for soldiery, gazed in amused and contemptuous silence as we passed. Children looked at us in wide-eyed wonder. Only the dumb beasts were demonstrative, and they in a manner which was not at all to our liking. Dogs barked, and sedate old family horses, which would stand placidly at the curbing while fire engines thundered past with bells clanging and sirens shrieking, pricked up their ears at our approach, and, after one startled glance, galloped madly away and disappeared in clouds of dust far in the distance.

We knew why the nursemaids were cool, and why family horses developed hysteria with such startling suddenness. But in our pride we did not see that which we did not wish to see. Therefore we marched, or, to be more truthful, shambled on, shouting lusty choruses with an air of boisterous gayety which was anything but genuine.

"You do as I do and you'll do right,
 Fall in and follow me!"

was a favorite with number 12 platoon. Their enthusiasm might have carried conviction had it not been for their personal appearance, which certainly did not. Number 15 platoon would strive manfully for a hearing with

"Steadily, shoulder to shoulder,
Steadily, blade by blade;
Marching along,
Sturdy and strong,
Like the boys of the old brigade."

As a strictly accurate historian I must confess that none of these assertions were quite true. We marched neither steadily, nor shoulder to shoulder, nor blade by blade. We straggled all over the road, and kept step only when the sergeant major doubled forward, warning us, with threats of extra drills, to keep in our fours or to "pick it up!" In fact, "the boys of the old brigade," whoever they may have been, would have scornfully repudiated the suggestion that we resembled them in any respect.

They would have been justified in doing so had any of them seen us at the end of six weeks of training. For, however reluctantly, we were forced to admit that Sergeant Harris was right when he called us "a raw batch o' rookies." Unpromising we were not. There was good stuff in the ranks, the material from which real soldiers are made, and were made; but it had not yet been rounded into shape. We were still nothing more than a homogeneous assembly of individuals.

We declined to accept the responsibility for the seeming slowness of our progress. We threw it unhesitatingly upon the War Office, which had not equipped us in a manner befitting our new station in life. Although we were recruited immediately after the outbreak of war, less than half of our number had been provided with uniforms. Many still wore their old civilian clothing. Others were dressed in canvas fatigue suits, or the worn-out uniforms of policemen and tramcar conductors. Every old-clothes shop on Petticoat Lane must have contributed its allotment of cast-off apparel.

Our arms and equipment were of an equally nondescript character. We might easily have been mistaken for a mob of vagrants which had pillaged a seventeenth-century arsenal. With a few slight changes in costuming for the sake of historical fidelity, we would have served as a citizen army for a realistic motion-picture drama depicting an episode in the French Revolution.

We derived what comfort we could from the knowledge that we were but one of many battalions of Kitchener's first hundred thousand equipped in this same makeshift fashion. We did not need the repeated assurances of cabinet ministers that England was not prepared for war. We were in a position to know that she was not. Otherwise, there had been an unpardonable lack of foresight in high places. Supplies came in driblets. Each night, when parades for the day were over, there was a rush for the orderly room bulletin board, which was scanned eagerly for news of an early issue of clothing. As likely as not we were disappointed, but occasionally jaded hopes revived.

"Number 15 platoon will parade at 4 P.M. on Thursday, the 24th, for boots, puttees, braces, and service dress caps."

Number 15 is our platoon. Promptly at the hour set we halt and right-turn in front of the Quartermaster Stores marquee. The quartermaster is there with pencil and notebook, and immediately takes charge of the proceedings.

"All men needing boots, one pace step forward, March!"

The platoon, sixty-five strong, steps forward as one man.

"All men needing braces, one pace step back, March!"

Again we move as a unit. The quartermaster hesitates for a moment; but he is a resourceful man and has been through this many times before. We all need boots, quite right! But the question is, Who need them most? Undoubtedly those whose feet are most in evidence through worn soles and tattered uppers. Adopting this sight test, he eliminates more than half the platoon, whereupon, by a further process of elimination, due to the fact that he has only sizes 7 and 8, he selects the fortunate twelve who are to walk dry shod.

The same method of procedure is carried out in selecting the braces. Private Reynolds, whose trousers are held in place by a wonderful mechanism composed of shoe-laces and bits of string, receives a pair; likewise, Private Stenebras, who, with the aid of safety pins, has fashioned coat and trousers into an ingenious one-piece garment. Caps and puttees are distributed with like impartiality, and we dismiss, the unfortunate ones growling and grumbling in discreet undertones until the platoon commander is out of hearing, whereupon the murmurs of discontent become loudly articulate.

"Kitchener's Rag-Time Army I calls it!" growls the veteran of South African fame. "Ain't we a 'andsome lot o' pozzie wallopers? Service? We ain't never a-go'n' to see service! You blokes won't, but watch me! I'm a-go'n' to grease off out o' this mob!"

No one remonstrated with this deservedly unpopular reservist when he grumbled about the shortage of supplies. He voiced the general sentiment. We all felt that we would like to "grease off" out of it. Our deficiencies in clothing and equipment were met by the Government with what seemed to us amazing slowness. However, Tommy is a sensible man. He realized that England had a big contract to fulfill, and that the first duty was to provide for the armies in the field. France, Russia, Belgium, all were looking to England for supplies. Kitchener's Mob must wait, trusting to the genius for organization, the faculty for getting things done, of its great and worthy chief, K. of K.

*   *   *   *   *   *

Our housing accommodations, throughout the autumn and winter of 1914-15, when England was in such urgent need of shelter for her rapidly increasing armies, were also of the makeshift order. We slept in leaky tents or in hastily constructed wooden shelters, many of which were afterward condemned by the medical inspectors. St. Martin's Plain, Shorncliffe, was an ideal camping-site for pleasant summer weather. But when the autumnal rains set in, the green pasture land became a quagmire. Mud was the great reality of our lives, the malignant deity which we fell down (in) and propitiated with profane rites. It was a thin, watery mud or a thick, viscous mud, as the steady downpour increased or diminished. Late in November we were moved to a city of wooden huts at Sandling Junction, to make room for newly recruited units. The dwellings were but half-finished, the drains were open ditches, and the rains descended and the floods came as usual. We lived an amphibious and wretched existence until January, when, to our great joy, we were transferred to billets in the Metropole, one of Folkestone's most fashionable hotels. To be sure, we slept on bare floors, but the roof was rainproof, which was the essential thing. The aesthetically inclined could lie in their blankets at night, gazing at richly gilded mirrors over the mantelpieces and beautifully frescoed ceilings refurnishing our apartments in all their former splendor. Private Henry Morgan was not of this type. Henry came in one evening rather the worse for liquor and with clubbed musket assaulted his unlovely reflection in an expensive mirror. I believe he is still paying for his lack of restraint at the rate of a sixpence per day, and will have canceled his obligation by January, 1921, if the war continues until that time.

*   *   *   *   *   *

Although we were poorly equipped and sometimes wretchedly housed, the commissariat was excellent and on the most generous scale from the very beginning. Indeed, there was nearly as much food wasted as eaten. Naturally, the men made no complaint, although they regretted seeing such quantities of food thrown daily into the refuse barrels. I often felt that something should be done about it. Many exposes were, in fact, written from all parts of England. It was irritating to read of German efficiency in the presence of England's extravagant and unbusinesslike methods. Tommy would say, "Lor, lummy! Ain't we got no pigs in England? That there food won't be wasted. We'll be eatin' it in sausages w'en we goes acrost the Channel"; whereupon he dismissed the whole question from his mind. This seemed to me then the typical Anglo-Saxon attitude. Everywhere there was waste, muddle-headedness, and apparently it was nobody's business, nobody's concern. Camps were sited in the wrong places and buildings erected only to be condemned. Tons of food were purchased overseas, transported across thousands of miles of ocean, only to be thrown into refuse barrels. The Government was robbed by avaricious hotel-keepers who made and were granted absurd claims for damages done to their property by billeted troops. But with vast new armies, recruited overnight, it is not strange that there should be mismanagement and friction at first. As the months passed, there was a marked change for the better. British efficiency asserted itself. This was made evident to us in scores of ways--the distribution of supplies, the housing and equipping of troops, their movements from one training area to another. At the last, we could only marvel that a great and complicated military machine had been so admirably and quickly perfected.

* * * * * *

Meanwhile our rigorous training continued from week to week in all weathers, even the most inclement. Reveille sounded at daybreak. For an hour before breakfast we did Swedish drill, a system of gymnastics which brought every lazy and disused muscle into play. Two hours daily were given to musketry practice. We were instructed in the description and recognition of targets, the use of cover, but chiefly in the use of our rifles. Through constant handling they became a part of us, a third arm which we grew to use quite instinctively. We fired the recruit's, and later, the trained soldier's course in musketry on the rifle ranges at Hythe and Aldershot, gradually improving our technique, until we were able to fire with some accuracy, fifteen rounds per minute. When we had achieved this difficult feat, we ceased to be recruits. We were skilled soldiers of the proud and illustrious order known as "England's Mad-Minute Men." After musketry practice, the remainder of the day was given to extended order, company, and battalion drill. Twice weekly we route-marched from ten to fifteen miles; and at night, after the parades for the day were finished, boxing and wrestling contests, arranged and encouraged by our officers, kept the red blood pounding through our bodies until "lights out" sounded at nine o'clock.

The character of our training changed as we progressed. We were done with squad, platoon, and company drill. Then came field maneuvers, attacks in open formation upon intrenched positions, finishing always with terrific bayonet charges. There were mimic battles, lasting all day, with from ten to twenty thousand men on each side. Artillery, infantry, cavalry, air craft--every branch of army service, in fact--had a share in these exciting field days when we gained bloodless victories or died painless and easy deaths at the command of red-capped field judges. We rushed boldly to the charge, shouting lustily, each man striving to be first at the enemy's position, only to be intercepted by a staff officer on horseback, staying the tide of battle with uplifted hand.

"March your men back, officer! You're out of action! My word! You've made a beastly mess of it! You're not on church parade, you know! You advanced across the open for three quarters of a mile in close column of platoons! Three batteries of field artillery and four machine guns have blown you to blazes! You haven't a man left!"

Sometimes we reached our objective with less fearful slaughter, but at the moment when there should have been the sharp clash and clang of steel on steel, the cries and groans of men fighting for their lives, we heard the bugles from far and near, sounding the "stand by," and friend and enemy dropped wearily to the ground for a rest while our officers assembled in conference around the motor of the divisional general.

All this was playing at war, and Tommy was "fed up" with play. As we marched back to barracks after a long day of monotonous field maneuvers, he eased his mind by making sarcastic comments upon this inconclusive kind of warfare. He began to doubt the good faith of the War Office in calling ours a "service" battalion. As likely as not we were for home defense and would never be sent abroad.

"Left! Right! Left! Right!
Why did I join the army?
Oh! Why did I ever join Kitchener's Mob?
Lor lummy! I must 'ave been balmy!"--

became the favorite, homeward-bound marching song. And so he "groused" and grumbled after the manner of Tommies the world over. And in the mean time he was daily approaching more nearly the standard of efficiency set by England's inexorable War Lord.

*   *   *   *   *   *

It was interesting to note the physical improvement in the men wrought by a life of healthy, well-ordered routine. My battalion was recruited largely from what is known in England as "the lower middle classes." There were shop assistants, clerks, railway and city employees, tradesmen, and a generous sprinkling of common laborers. Many of them had been used to indoor life, practically all of them to city life, and needed months of the hardest kind of training before they could be made physically fit, before they could be seasoned and toughened to withstand the hardships of active service.

Plenty of hard work in the open air brought great and welcome changes. The men talked of their food, anticipated it with a zest which came from realizing, for the first time, the joy of being genuinely hungry. They watched their muscles harden with the satisfaction known to every normal man when he is becoming physically efficient. Food, exercise, and rest, taken in wholesome quantities and at regular intervals, were having the usual excellent results. For my own part, I had never before been in such splendid health. I wished that it might at all times be possible for democracies to exercise a beneficent paternalism over the lives of their citizenry, at least in matters of health. It seems a great pity that the principle of personal freedom should be responsible for so many ill-shaped and ill-sorted physical incompetents. My fellow Tommies were living, really living, for the first time. They had never before known what it means to be radiantly, buoyantly healthy.

There were, as well, more profound and subtle changes in thoughts and habits. The restraints of discipline and the very exacting character of military life and training gave them self-control, mental alertness. At the beginning, they were individuals, no more cohesive than so many grains of wet sand. After nine months of training they acted as a unit, obeying orders with that instinctive promptness of action which is so essential on the field of battle when men think scarcely at all. But it is true that what was their gain as soldiers was, to a certain extent, their loss as individuals. When we went on active service I noted that men who were excellent followers were not infrequently lost when called upon for independent action.

They had not been trained to take the initiative, and had become so accustomed to having their thinking done for them that they often became confused and excited when they had to do it for themselves.

Discipline was an all-important factor in the daily grind. At the beginning of their training, the men of the new armies were gently dealt with. Allowances were made for civilian frailties and shortcomings. But as they adapted themselves to changed conditions, restrictions became increasingly severe. Old privileges disappeared one by one. Individual liberty became a thing of the past. The men resented this bitterly for a time. Fierce hatreds of officers and N.C.O.s were engendered and there was much talk of revenge when we should get to the front. I used to look forward with misgiving to that day. It seemed probable that one night in the trenches would suffice for a wholesale slaughtering of officers. Old scores were to be paid off, old grudges wiped out with our first issue of ball ammunition. Many a fist-banged board at the wet canteen gave proof of Tommy's earnestness.

"Shoot 'im?" he would say, rattling the beer glasses the whole length of the table with a mighty blow of his fist. "Blimy! Wite! That's all you got to do! Just wite till we get on the other side!"

But all these threats were forgotten months before the time came for carrying them out. Once Tommy understood the reasonableness of severe discipline, he took his punishment for his offenses without complaint. He realized, too, the futility of kicking against the pricks. In the army he belonged to the Government body and soul. He might resent its treatment of him. He might behave like a sulky schoolboy, disobey order after order, and break rule after rule. In that case he found himself check-mated at every turn. Punishment became more and more severe. No one was at all concerned about his grievances. He might become an habitual offender from sheer stupidity, but in doing so, he injured no one but himself.

A few of these incorrigibles were discharged in disgrace. A few followed the lead of the Boer warrior. After many threats which we despaired of his ever carrying out, he finally "greased off." He was immediately posted as a deserter, but to our great joy was never captured. With the disappearance of the malcontents and incorrigibles the battalion soon reached a high grade of efficiency. The physical incompetents were likewise ruthlessly weeded out. All of us had passed a fairly thorough examination at the recruiting offices; but many had physical defects which were discovered only by the test of actual training. In the early days of the war, requirements were much more severe than later, when England learned how great would be the need for men. Many, who later reenlisted in other regiments, were discharged as "physically unfit for further military service."

If the standard of conduct in my battalion is any criterion, then I can say truthfully that there is very little crime in Lord Kitchener's armies either in England or abroad. The "jankers" or defaulters' squad was always rather large; but the "jankers men" were offenders against minor points in discipline. Their crimes were untidy appearance on parade, inattention in the ranks, tardiness at roll-call, and others of the sort, all within the jurisdiction of a company officer. The punishment meted out varied according to the seriousness of the offense, and the past-conduct record of the offender. It usually consisted of from one to ten days, "C.B."--confined to barracks. During the period of his sentence the offender was forbidden to leave camp after the parades for the day were ended. And in order that he might have no opportunity to do so, he was compelled to answer his name at the guard-room whenever it should be sounded.

Only twice in England did we have a general court-martial, the offense in each case being assault by a private upon an N.C.O., and the penalty awarded, three months in the military prison at Aldershot. Tommy was quiet and law-abiding in England, his chief lapses being due to an exaggerated estimate of his capacity for beer. In France, his conduct, in so far as my observation goes, has been splendid throughout. During six months in the trenches I saw but two instances of drunkenness. Although I witnessed nearly everything which took place in my own battalion, and heard the general gossip of many others, never did I see or hear of a woman treated otherwise than courteously. Neither did I see or hear of any instances of looting or petty pilfering from the civilian inhabitants. It is true that the men had fewer opportunities for misconduct, and they were fighting in a friendly country. Even so, active service as we found it was by no means free from temptations. The admirable restraint of most of the men in the face of them was a fine thing to see.

Frequent changes were made in methods of training in England, to correspond with changing conditions of modern warfare as exemplified in the trenches. Textbooks on military tactics and strategy, which were the inspired gospel of the last generation of soldiers, became obsolete overnight. Experience gained in Indian

Mutiny wars or on the veldt in South Africa was of little value in the trenches in Flanders. The emphasis shifted from open fighting to trench warfare, and the textbook which our officers studied was a typewritten serial issued semiweekly by the War Office, and which was based on the dearly bought experience of officers at the front.

We spent many a starry night on the hills above Folkestone digging trenches and building dug-outs according to General Staff instructions, and many a rainy one we came home, covered with mud, but happy in the thought that we were approximating, as nearly as could be, the experience of the boys at the front. Bomb-throwing squads were formed, and the best shots in the battalion, the men who had made marksmen's scores on the rifle ranges, were given daily instruction in the important business of sniping. More generous provision for the training of machine-gun teams was made, but so great was the lack in England of these important weapons, that for many weeks we drilled with wooden substitutes, gaining such knowledge of machine gunnery as we could from the study of our M.G. manuals.

These new duties, coming as an addition to our other work, meant an increased period of training. We were impatient to be at the front, but we realized by this time that Lord Kitchener was serious in his demand that the men of the new armies be efficiently trained. Therefore we worked with a will, and at last, after nine months of monotonous toil, the order came. We were to proceed on active service.

CHAPTER IV
ORDERED ABROAD

One Sunday morning in May we assembled on the barrack square at Aldershot for the last time. Every man was in full marching order. His rifle was the "Short Lee Enfield, Mark IV," his bayonet, the long single-edged blade in general use throughout the British Army. In addition to his arms he carried 120 rounds of ".303" caliber ammunition, an intrenching-tool, water-bottle, haversack, containing both emergency and the day's rations, and his pack, strapped to shoulders and waist in such a way that the weight of it was equally distributed. His pack contained the following articles: A greatcoat, a woolen shirt, two or three pairs of socks, a change of underclothing, a "housewife,"--the soldiers' sewing-kit,--a towel, a cake of soap, and a "hold-all," in which were a knife, fork, spoon, razor, shaving-brush, toothbrush, and comb. All of these were useful and sometimes essential articles, particularly the toothbrush, which Tommy regarded as the best little instrument for cleaning the mechanism of a rifle ever invented. Strapped on top of the pack was the blanket roll wrapped in a waterproof ground sheet; and hanging beneath it, the canteen in its khaki-cloth cover. Each man wore an identification disk on a cord about his neck. It was stamped with his name, regimental number, regiment, and religion. A first-aid field dressing, consisting of an antiseptic gauze pad and bandage and a small vial of iodine, sewn in the lining of his tunic, completed the equipment.

Physically, the men were "in the pink," as Tommy says. They were clear-eyed, vigorous, alert, and as hard as nails. With their caps on, they looked the well-trained soldiers which they were; but with caps removed, they resembled so many uniformed convicts less the prison pallor. "Oversea haircuts" were the last tonsorial cry, and for several days previous to our departure, the army hairdressers had been busily wielding the close-cutting clippers.

Each of us had received a copy of Lord Kitchener's letter to the troops ordered abroad, a brief, soldierlike statement of the standard of conduct which England expected of her fighting men:--

> You are ordered abroad as a soldier of the King to help our French comrades against the invasion of a common enemy. You have to perform a task which will need your courage, your energy, your patience. Remember that the honor of the British Army depends upon your individual conduct. It will be your duty not only to set an example of discipline and perfect steadiness under fire, but also to maintain the most friendly relations with those whom you are helping in this struggle. The operations in which you are engaged will, for the most part, take place in a friendly country, and you can do your own country no better service than in showing yourself, in France and Belgium, in the true character of a British soldier.
> Be invariably courteous, considerate, and kind. Never do anything likely to injure or destroy property, and always look upon looting as a disgraceful act. You are sure to meet with a welcome and to be trusted; and your conduct must justify that welcome and that trust. Your duty cannot be done unless your health is sound. So keep constantly on your guard against any excesses. In this new experience you may find temptations both in wine and women. You must entirely resist both temptations, and while treating all women with perfect courtesy, you should avoid any intimacy.
>
>   Do your duty bravely.
>   Fear God.
>   Honor the King.
>
> Kitchener,
> Field-Marshal.

It was an effective appeal and a constant reminder to the men of the glorious traditions of the British Army. In the months that followed, I had opportunity to learn how deep and lasting was the impression made upon them by Lord Kitchener's first, and I believe his only, letter to his soldiers.

The machinery for moving troops in England works without the slightest friction. The men, transport, horses, commissariat, medical stores, and supplies of a battalion are entrained in less than half an hour. Everything is timed to the minute. Battalion after battalion and train after train, we moved out of Aldershot at half-hour intervals. Each train arrived at the port of embarkation on schedule time and pulled up on the docks by the side of a troop transport, great slate-colored liners taken out of the merchant service. Not a moment was lost. The last man was aboard and the last wagon on the crane swinging up over the ship's side as the next train came in.

Ship by ship we moved down the harbor in the twilight, the boys crowding the rail on both sides, taking their farewell look at England--home. It was the last farewell for many of them, but there was no martial music, no waving of flags, no tearful good-byes. Our farewell was as prosaic as our long period of training had been. We were each one a very small part of a tremendous business organization which works without any of the display considered so essential in the old days.

We left England without a cheer. There was not so much as a wave of the hand from the wharf; for there was no one on the wharf to wave, with the exception of a few dock laborers, and they had seen too many soldiers off to the front to be sentimental about it. It was a tense moment for the men, but trust Tommy to relieve a tense situation. As we steamed away from the landing slip, we passed a barge, loaded to the water's edge with coal. Tommy has a song pat to every occasion. He enjoys, above all things, giving a ludicrous twist to a "weepy" ballad. When we were within hailing distance of the coal barge, he began singing one of this variety, "Keep the Home Fires Burning," to those smutty-faced barge hands. Every one joined in heartily, forgetting all about the solemnity of the leave-taking.

Tommy is a prosaic chap. This was never more apparent to me than upon that pleasant evening in May when we said good-bye to England. The lights of home were twinkling their farewells far in the distance. Every moment brought us nearer to the great adventure. We were "off to the wars," to take our places in the far-flung battle line. Here was Romance lavishly offering gifts dearest to the hearts of Youth, offering them to clerks, barbers, tradesmen, drapers' assistants, men who had never known an adventure more thrilling than a holiday excursion to the Isle of Man or a week of cycling in Kent. And they accepted them with all the stolidity native to Englishmen. The eyes of the world were upon them. They had become the knights-errant of every schoolgirl. They were figures of heroic proportions to every one but themselves.

French soldiers are conscious of the romantic possibilities offered them by the so-called "divine accident of war." They go forth to fight for Glorious France, France the Unconquerable! Tommy shoulders his rifle and departs for the four corners of the world on a "bloomin' fine little 'oliday!" A railway journey and a sea voyage in one! "Blimy! Not 'arf bad, wot?" Perhaps he is stirred at the thought of fighting for "England, Home, and Beauty." Perhaps he does thrill inwardly, remembering a sweetheart left behind. But he keeps it jolly well to himself. He has read me many of his letters home, some of them written during an engagement which will figure prominently in the history of the great World War. "Well, I can't think of anything more now," threads its way through a meager page of commonplaces about the weather, his food, and his personal health. A frugal line of cross-marks for kisses, at the bottom of the page, is his only concession to sentiment.

There was, however, one burst of enthusiasm, as we started on our journey, which struck me as being spontaneous, and splendid, and thoroughly English. Outside the harbor we were met by our guardians, a fleet of destroyers which was to give us safe convoy across the Channel. The moment they saw them the men broke forth into prolonged cheering, and there were glad shouts of--

"There they are, me lads! There's some o' the little old watch dogs wot's keepin' 'em bottled up!"

"Good old navy! That's w'ere we got 'em by the throat!"

"Let's give 'em 'Sons of the Sea!'"

And they did. They sang with a spirit of exaltation which Englishmen rarely betray, and which convinced me how nearly the sea and England's position as Mistress of the Seas touch the Englishman's heart of hearts.

"Sons of the sea,
All British born,
Sailing the ocean,
Laughing foes to scorn.
They may build their ships, my lads,
And think they know the game;
But they can't beat the boys of the bulldog breed
Who made old England's name!"

It was a confession of faith. On the sea England can't be beaten. Tommy believes that with his whole soul, and on this occasion he sang with all the warmth of religious conviction.

Our Channel voyage was uneventful. Each transport was guarded by two destroyers, one on either side, the three vessels keeping abreast and about fifty yards apart during the entire journey. The submarine menace was then at its height, and we were prepared for an emergency. The boats were swung ready for immediate launching, and all of the men were provided with life-preservers. But England had been transporting troops and supplies to the firing-line for so many months without accident that none of us were at all concerned about the possibility of danger. Furthermore, the men were too busy studying "Tommy Atkins's French Manual" to think about submarines. They were putting the final polish on their accent in preparation for to-morrow's landing.

"Alf, 'ow's this: 'Madamaselly, avay vu dee pang?'"

"Wot do you s'y for 'Gimme a tuppenny packet o' Nosegay'?"

"'Bonjoor, Monseer!' That ain't so dusty, Freddie, wot?"

"Let's try that Marcelase again. You start it, 'Arry."

"Let Nobby. 'E knows the sounds better'n wot I do."

"'It 'er up, Nobby! We gotta learn that so we can sing it on the march."

"Wite till I find it in me book. All right now--

   Allons infants dee la Pat-ree,   La joor de glory is arrivay."

Such bits of conversation may be of little interest, but they have the merit of being genuine. All of them were jotted down in my notebook at the times when I heard them.

The following day we crowded into the typical French army troop train, eight chevaux *or forty* hommes to a car, and started on a leisurely journey to the firing-line. We traveled all day, at eight or ten miles an hour, through Normandy. We passed through pleasant towns and villages lying silent in the afternoon sunshine, and seemingly almost deserted, and through the open country fragrant with the scent of apple blossoms. Now and then children waved to us from a cottage window, and in the fields old men and women and girls leaned silently on their hoes or their rakes and watched us pass. Occasionally an old reservist, guarding the railway line, would lift his cap and shout, "Vive l'Angleterre!" But more often he would lean on his rifle and smile, nodding his head courteously but silently to our salutations. Tommy, for all his stolid, dogged cheeriness, sensed the tragedy of France. It was a land swept bare of all its fine young manhood. There was no pleasant stir and bustle of civilian life. Those who were left went about their work silently and joylessly. When we asked of the men, we received, always, the same quiet, courteous reply: "A la guerre, monsieur."

The boys soon learned the meaning of the phrase, "a la guerre." It became a war-cry, a slogan. It was shouted back and forth from car to car and from train to train. You can imagine how eager we all were; how we strained our ears, whenever the train stopped, for the sound of the guns. But not until the following morning, when we reached the little village at the end of our railway journey, did we hear them, a low muttering like the sound of thunder beyond the horizon. How we cheered at the first faint sound which was to become so deafening, so terrible to us later! It was music to us then; for we were like the others who had gone that way. We knew nothing of war. We thought it must be something adventurous and fine. Something to make the blood leap and the heart sing. We marched through the village and down the poplar-lined road, surprised, almost disappointed, to see the neat, well-kept houses, and the pleasant, level fields, green with spring crops. We had expected that everything would be in ruins. At this stage of the journey, however, we were still some twenty-five miles from the firing-line.

During all the journey from the coast, we had seen, on every side, evidences of that wonderfully organized branch of the British military system, the Army Service Corps. From the village at which we detrained, everything was English. Long lines of motor transport lorries were parked along the sides of the roads. There were great ammunition bases, commissariat supply depots, motor repair shops, wheelwright and blacksmith shops, where one saw none but khaki-clad soldiers engaged in all the noncombatant business essential to the maintenance of large armies. There were long lines of transport wagons loaded with supplies, traveling field-kitchens, with chimneys smoking and kettles steaming as they bumped over the cobbled roads, water carts, Red Cross carts, motor ambulances, batteries of artillery, London omnibuses, painted slate gray, filled with troops, seemingly endless columns of infantry on foot, all moving with us, along parallel roads, toward the firing-line. And most of these troops and supply columns belonged to my own division, one small cog in the British fighting machine.

We advanced toward the war zone in easy stages. It was intensely hot, and the rough, cobbled roads greatly increased the difficulty of marching. In England we had frequently tramped from fifteen to twenty-five miles in a day without fatigue. But the roads there were excellent, and the climate moist and cool. Upon our first day's march in France, a journey of only nine miles, scores of men were overcome by the heat, and several died. The suffering of the men was so great, in fact, that a halt was made earlier than had been planned, and we bivouacked for the night in the fields.

Life with a battalion on the march proceeds with the same orderly routine as when in barracks. Every man has his own particular employment. Within a few moments, the level pasture land was converted into a busy community of a thousand inhabitants. We made serviceable little dwellings by lacing together two or three waterproof ground-sheets and erecting them on sticks or tying them to the wires of the fences. Latrines and refuse pits were dug under the supervision of the battalion medical officer. The sick were cared for and justice dispensed with the same thoroughness as in England. The day's offenders against discipline were punished with what seemed to us unusual severity. But we were now on active service, and offenses which were trivial in England were looked upon, for this reason, in the light of serious crimes.

Daily we approached a little nearer to our goal, sleeping, at night, in the open fields or in the lofts of great rambling farm-buildings. Most of these places had been used for soldiers' billets scores of times before. The walls were covered with the names of men and regiments, and there were many penciled suggestions as to the best place to go for a basin of "coffay oh lay," as Tommy called it. Every roadside cottage was, in fact, Tommy's tavern. The thrifty French peasant women kept open house for soldiers. They served us with delicious coffee and thick slices of French bread, for the very reasonable sum of twopence. They were always friendly and hospitable, and the men, in turn, treated them with courteous and kindly respect. Tommy was a great favorite with the French children. They climbed on his lap and rifled his pockets; and they delighted him by talking in his own vernacular, for they were quick to pick up English words and phrases. They sang "Tipperary" and "Rule Britannia," and "God Save the King," so quaintly and prettily that the men kept them at it for hours at a time.

And so, during a week of stifling heat, we moved slowly forward. The sound of the guns grew in intensity, from a faint rumbling to a subdued roar, until one evening, sitting in the open windows of a stable loft, we saw the far-off lightenings of bursting shells, and the trench rockets soaring skyward; and we heard bursts of rifle and machine-gun fire, very faintly, like the sound of chestnuts popping in an oven.

CHAPTER V
THE PARAPET-ETIC SCHOOL

"We're going in to-night."

The word was given out by the orderly sergeants at four in the afternoon. At 4.03 every one in camp had heard the news. Scores of miniature hand laundries, which were doing a thriving business down by the duck pond, immediately shut up shop. Damp and doubtfully clean ration bags, towels, and shirts which were draped along the fences, were hastily gathered together and thrust into the capacious depths of pack-sacks. Members of the battalion's sporting contingent broke up their games of tuppenny brag without waiting for "just one more hand," an unprecedented thing. The makers of war ballads, who were shouting choruses to the merry music of the mouth-organ band, stopped in the midst of their latest composition, and rushed off to get their marching order together. At 4.10 every one, with the exception of the officers' servants, was ready to move off. This, too, was unprecedented. Never before had we made haste more gladly or less needfully, but never before had there been such an incentive to haste. We were going into the trenches for the first time.

The officers' servants, commonly called "batmen," were unfortunate rankers who, in moments of weakness, had sold themselves into slavery for half a crown per week. The batman's duty is to make tea for his officer, clean his boots, wash his clothes, tuck him into bed at night, and make himself useful generally. The real test of a good batman, however, is his carrying capacity. In addition to his own heavy burden he must carry various articles belonging to his officer: enameled wash-basins, rubber boots, bottles of Apollinaris water, service editions of the modern English poets and novelists, spirit lamps, packages of food, boxes of cigars and cigarettes,--in fact, all of his personal luggage which is in excess of the allotted thirty-five pounds which is carried on the battalion transport wagons.

On this epoch-marking day, even the officers' servants were punctual. When the order, "Packs on! Fall in!" was given, not a man was missing. Every one was in harness, standing silently, expectantly, in his place.

"Charge magazines!"

The bolts clicked open with the sound of one as we loaded our rifles with ball ammunition. Five long shiny cartridges were slipped down the charger guide into the magazine, and the cut-off closed.

"Move off in column of route, 'A' company leading!"

We swung into the country road in the gathering twilight, and turned sharply to our left at the crossroad where the signboard read, "To the Firing-Line. For the Use of the Military Only."

Coming into the trenches for the first time when the deadlock along the western front had become seemingly unbreakable, we reaped the benefit of the experience of the gallant little remnant of the first British Expeditionary Force. After the retreat from Mons, they had dug themselves in and were holding tenaciously on, awaiting the long-heralded arrival of Kitchener's Mob. As the units of the new armies arrived in France, they were sent into the trenches for twenty-four hours' instruction in trench warfare, with a battalion of regulars. This one-day course in trench fighting is preliminary to fitting new troops into their own particular sectors along the front. The facetious subalterns called it "The Parapet-etic School." Months later, we ourselves became members of the faculty, but on this first occasion we were marching up as the meekest of undergraduates.

It was quite dark when we entered the desolate belt of country known as the "fire zone." Pipes and cigarettes were put out and talking ceased. We extended to groups of platoons in fours, at one hundred paces interval, each platoon keeping in touch with the one in front by means of connecting files. We passed rows of ruined cottages where only the scent of the roses in neglected little front gardens reminded one of the home-loving people who had lived there in happier days. Dim lights streamed through chinks and crannies in the walls. Now and then blanket coverings would be lifted from apertures that had been windows or doors, and we would see bright fires blazing in the middle of brick kitchen floors, and groups of men sitting about them luxuriously sipping tea from steaming canteens. They were laughing and talking and singing songs in loud, boisterous voices which contrasted strangely with our timid noiselessness. I was marching with one of the trench guides who had been sent back to pilot us to our position. I asked him if the Tommies in the houses were not in danger of being heard by the enemy. He laughed uproariously at this, whereupon one of our officers, a little second lieutenant, turned and hissed in melodramatic undertones, "Silence in the ranks there! Where do you think you are!" Officers and men, we were new to the game then, and we held rather exaggerated notions as to the amount of care to be observed in moving up to the trenches.

"Blimy, son!" whispered the trench guide, "you might think we was only a couple o' 'unnerd yards away from Fritzie's trenches! We're a good two an' a 'arf miles back 'ere. All right to be careful arter you gets closer up; but they's no use w'isperin' w'en you ain't even in rifle range."

With lights, of course, it was a different matter altogether. Can't be too careful about giving the enemy artillery an aiming mark. This was the reason all the doors and windows of the ruined cottages were so carefully blanketed.

"Let old Fritzie see a light,--"Ello!' 'e says, 'blokes in billets!' an' over comes a 'arf-dozen shells knockin' you all to blazes."

As we came within the range of rifle fire, we again changed our formation, and marched in single file along the edge of the road. The sharp crack! crack!= of small arms now sounded with vicious and ominous distinctness. We heard the melancholy song of the ricochets and spent bullets as they whirled in a wide arc, high over our heads, and occasionally the less pleasing phtt! phtt! of those speeding straight from the muzzle of a German rifle. We breathed more freely when we entered the communication trench in the center of a little thicket, a mile or more back of the first-line trenches.

We wound in and out of what appeared in the darkness to be a hopeless labyrinth of earthworks. Cross-streets and alleys led off in every direction. All along the way we had glimpses of dugouts lighted by candles, the doorways carefully concealed with blankets or pieces of old sacking. Groups of Tommies, in comfortable nooks and corners, were boiling tea or frying bacon over little stoves made of old iron buckets or biscuit tins.

I marveled at the skill of our trench guide who went confidently on in the darkness, with scarcely a pause. At length, after a winding, zigzag journey, we arrived at our trench where we met the Gloucesters.

There isn't one of us who hasn't a warm spot in his heart for the Gloucesters: they welcomed us so heartily and initiated us into all the mysteries of trench etiquette and trench tradition. We were, at best, but amateur Tommies. In them I recognized the lineal descendants of the line Atkins; men whose grandfathers had fought in the Crimea, and whose fathers in Indian mutinies. They were the fighting sons of fighting sires, and they taught us more of life in the trenches, in twenty-four hours, than we had learned during nine months of training in England. An infantryman of my company has a very kindly feeling toward one of them who probably saved his life before we had been in the trenches five minutes. Our first question was, of course, "How far is it to the German lines?" and in his eagerness to see, my fellow Tommy jumped up on the firing-bench for a look, with a lighted cigarette in his mouth. He was pulled down into the trench just as a rifle cracked and a bullet went zing-g-g from the parapet precisely where he had been standing. Then the Gloucester gave him a friendly little lecture which none of us afterward forgot.

"Now, look 'ere, son! Never get up for a squint at Fritz with a fag on! 'E's got every sandbag along this parapet numbered, same as we've got 'is. 'Is snipers is a-layin' fer us same as ours is a-layin' fer 'im." Then, turning to the rest of us, "Now, we ain't arskin' to 'ave no burial parties. But if any of you blokes wants to be the stiff, stand up w'ere this guy lit the gas."

There weren't any takers, and a moment later another bullet struck a sandbag in the same spot.

"See? 'E spotted you. 'E'll keep a-pottin' away at that place for an hour, 'opin' to catch you lookin' over again. Less see if we can find 'im. Give us that biscuit tin, 'Enery."

Then we learned the biscuit-tin-finder trick for locating snipers. It's only approximate, of course, but it gives a pretty good hint at the direction from which the shots come. It doesn't work in the daytime, for a sniper is too clever to fire at it. But a biscuit tin, set on the parapet at night in a badly sniped position, is almost certain to be hit. The angle from which the shots come is shown by the jagged edges of tin around the bullet holes. Then, as the Gloucester said, "Give 'im a nice little April shower out o' yer machine gun in that direction. You may fetch 'im. But if you don't, 'e won't bother you no more fer an hour or two."

We learned how orders are passed down the line, from sentry to sentry, quietly, and with the speed of a man running. We learned how the sentries are posted and their duties. We saw the intricate mazes of telephone wires, and the men of the signaling corps at their posts in the trenches, in communication with brigade, divisional, and army corps headquarters. We learned how to "sleep" five men in a four-by-six dugout; and, when there are no dugouts, how to hunch up on the firing-benches with our waterproof sheets over our heads, and doze, with our knees for a pillow. We learned the order of precedence for troops in the communication trenches.

"Never forget that! Outgoin' troops 'as the right o' way. They ain't 'ad no rest, an' they're all slathered in mud, likely, an' dead beat fer sleep. Incomin' troops is fresh, an' they stands to one side to let the others pass."

We saw the listening patrols go out at night, through the underground passage which leads to the far side of the barbed-wire entanglements. From there they creep far out between the opposing lines of trenches, to keep watch upon the movements of the enemy, and to report the presence of his working parties or patrols. This is dangerous, nerve-trying work, for the men sent out upon it are exposed not only to the shots of the enemy, but to the wild shots of their own comrades as well. I saw one patrol come in just before dawn. One of the men brought with him a piece of barbed wire, clipped from the German entanglements two hundred and fifty yards away.

"Taffy, 'ave a look at this 'ere. Three-ply stuff wot you can 'ardly get yer nippers through. 'Ad to saw an' saw, an' w'en I all but 'ad it, lummy! if they didn't send up a rocket wot bleedin' near 'it me in the 'ead!"

"Tyke it to Captain Stevens. I 'eard 'im s'y 'e's wantin' a bit to show to one of the artill'ry blokes. 'E's got a bet on with 'im that it's three-ply wire. Now, don't forget, Bobby! Touch 'im fer a couple o' packets o' fags!"

I was tremendously interested. At that time it seemed incredible to me that men crawled over to the German lines in this manner and clipped pieces of German wire for souvenirs.

"Did you hear anything?" I asked him.

"'Eard a flute some Fritzie was a-playin' of. An' you ought to 'ave 'eard 'em a-singin'! Doleful as 'ell!"

Several men were killed and wounded during the night. One of them was a sentry with whom I had been talking only a few moments before. He was standing on the firing-bench looking out into the darkness, when he fell back into the trench without a cry. It was a terrible wound. I would not have believed that a bullet could so horribly disfigure one. He was given first aid by the light of a candle; but it was useless. Silently his comrades removed his identification disk and wrapped him in a blanket. "Poor old Walt!" they said. An hour later he was buried in a shell hole at the back of the trench.

One thing we learned during our first night in the trenches was of the very first importance. And that was, respect for our enemies. We came from England full of absurd newspaper tales about the German soldier's inferiority as a fighting man. We had read that he was a wretched marksman: he would not stand up to the bayonet: whenever opportunity offered he crept over and gave himself up: he was poorly fed and clothed and was so weary of the war that his officers had to drive him to fight, at the muzzles of their revolvers. We thought him almost beneath contempt. We were convinced in a night that we had greatly underestimated his abilities as a marksman. As for his all-round inferiority as a fighting man, one of the Gloucesters put it rather well:--

"'Ere! If the Germans is so bloomin' rotten, 'ow is it we ain't a-fightin' 'em sommers along the Rhine, or in Austry-Hungry? No, they ain't a-firin' wild, I give you my word! Not around this part o' France they ain't! Wot do you s'y, Jerry?"

Jerry made a most illuminating contribution to the discussion of Fritz as a fighting man:--

"I'll tell you wot! If ever I gets through this 'ere war; if I 'as the luck to go 'ome again, with me eyesight, I'll never feel syfe w'en I sees a Fritzie, unless I'm a-lookin' at 'im through me periscope from be'ind a bit o' cover."

* * * * * *

How am I to give a really vivid picture of trench life as I saw it for the first time, how make it live for others, when I remember that the many descriptive accounts I had read of it in England did not in the least visualize it for me? I watched the rockets rising from the German lines, watched them burst into points of light, over the devastated strip of country called "No-Man's-Land" and drift slowly down. And I watched the charitable shadows rush back like the very wind of darkness. The desolate landscape emerged from the gloom and receded again, like a series of pictures thrown upon a screen. All of this was so new, so terrible, I doubted its reality. Indeed, I doubted my own identity, as one does at times when brought face to face with some experiences which cannot be compared with past experiences or even measured by them. I groped darkly, for some new truth which was flickering just beyond the border of consciousness. But I was so blinded by the glamour of the adventure that it did not come to me then. Later I understood. It was my first glimmering realization of the tremendous sadness, the awful futility of war.

CHAPTER VI
PRIVATE HOLLOWAY, PROFESSOR OF HYGIENE

The following morning we wandered through the trenches listening to the learned discourse of the genial professors of the Parapet-etic School, storing up much useful information for future reference. I made a serious blunder when I asked one of them a question about Ypres, for I pronounced the name French fashion, which put me under suspicion as a "swanker."

"Don't try to come it, son," he said. "S'y 'Wipers.' That's wot we calls it."

Henceforth it was "Wipers" for me, although I learned that "Eeps" and "Yipps" are sanctioned by some trench authorities. I made no further mistakes of this nature, and by keeping silent about the names of the towns and villages along our front, I soon learned the accepted pronunciation of all of them. Armentieres is called "Armenteers"; Balleul, "Bally-all"; Hazebrouck, "Hazy-Brook"; and what more natural than "Plug-Street," Atkinsese for Ploegsteert?

As was the case wherever I went, my accent betrayed my American birth; and again, as an American Expeditionary Force of one, I was shown many favors. Private Shorty Holloway, upon learning that I was a "Yank," offered to tell me "every bloomin' thing about the trenches that a bloke needs to know." I was only too glad to place myself under his instruction.

"Right you are!" said Shorty; "now, sit down 'ere w'ile I'm goin' over me shirt, an' arsk me anything yer a mind to." I began immediately by asking him what he meant by "going over" his shirt.

"Blimy! You are new to this game, mate! You mean to s'y you ain't got any graybacks!"

I confessed shamefacedly that I had not. He stripped to the waist, turned his shirt wrong side out, and laid it upon his knee.

"'Ave a look," he said proudly.

The less said about my discoveries the better for the fastidiously minded. Suffice it to say that I made my first acquaintance with members of a British Expeditionary Force which is not mentioned in official communiques.

"Trench pets," said Shorty. Then he told me that they were not all graybacks. There is a great variety of species, but they all belong to the same parasitical family, and wage a non-discriminating warfare upon the soldiery on both sides of No-man's-Land. Germans, British, French, Belgians alike were their victims.

"You'll soon 'ave plenty," he said reassuringly; "I give you about a week to get covered with 'em. Now, wot you want to do is this: always 'ave an extra shirt in yer pack. Don't be a bloomin' ass an' sell it fer a packet o' fags like I did! An' the next time you writes to England, get some one to send you out some Keatings"--he displayed a box of grayish-colored powder. "It won't kill 'em, mind you! They ain't nothin' but fire that'll kill 'em. But Keatings tykes all the ginger out o' 'em. They ain't near so lively arter you strafe 'em with this 'ere powder."

I remembered Shorty's advice later when I became a reluctant host to a prolific colony of graybacks. For nearly six months I was never without a box of Keatings, and I was never without the need for it.

Barbed wire had a new and terrible significance for me from the first day which we spent in the trenches. I could more readily understand why there had been so long a deadlock on the western front. The entanglements in front of the first line of trenches were from fifteen to twenty yards wide, the wires being twisted from post to post in such a hopeless jumble that no man could possibly get through them under fire. The posts were set firmly in the ground, but there were movable segments, every fifty or sixty yards, which could be put to one side in case an attack was to be launched against the German lines.

At certain positions there were what appeared to be openings through the wire, but these were nothing less than man-traps which have been found serviceable in case of an enemy attack. In an assault men follow the line of least resistance when they reach the barbed wire. These apparent openings are V-shaped, with the open end toward the enemy. The attacking troops think they see a clear passageway. They rush into the trap, and when it is filled with struggling men, machine guns are turned upon them, and, as Shorty said, "You got 'em cold."

That, at least, was the presumption. Practically, man-traps were not always a success. The intensive bombardments which precede infantry attacks play havoc with entanglements, but there is always a chance of the destruction being incomplete, as upon one occasion farther north, where, Shorty told me, a man-trap caught a whole platoon of Germans "dead to rights."

"But this is wot gives you the pip," he said. "'Ere we got three lines of trenches, all of 'em wired up so that a rat couldn't get through without scratchin' hisself to death. Fritzie's got better wire than wot we 'ave, an' more of it. An' 'e's got more machine guns, more artill'ry, more shells. They ain't any little old man-killer ever invented wot they 'aven't got more of than we 'ave. An' at 'ome they're a-s'yin', 'W'y don't they get on with it? W'y don't they smash through?' Let some of 'em come out 'ere an' 'ave a try! That's all I got to s'y."

I didn't tell Shorty that I had been, not exactly an armchair critic, but at least a barrack-room critic in England. I had wondered why British and French troops had failed to smash through. A few weeks in the trenches gave me a new viewpoint. I could only wonder at the magnificent fighting qualities of soldiers who had held their own so effectively against armies equipped and armed and munitioned as the Germans were.

After he had finished drugging his trench pets, Shorty and I made a tour of the trenches. I was much surprised at seeing how clean and comfortable they can be kept in pleasant summer weather. Men were busily at work sweeping up the walks, collecting the rubbish, which was put into sandbags hung on pegs at intervals along the fire trench. At night the refuse was taken back of the trenches and buried. Most of this work devolved upon the pioneers whose business it was to keep the trenches sanitary.

The fire trench was built in much the same way as those which we had made during our training in England. In pattern it was something like a tesselated border. For the space of five yards it ran straight, then it turned at right angles around a traverse of solid earth six feet square, then straight again for another five yards, then around another traverse, and so throughout the length of the line. Each five-yard segment, which is called a "bay," offered firing room for five men. The traverses, of course, were for the purpose of preventing enfilade fire. They also limited the execution which might be done by one shell. Even so they were not an unmixed blessing, for they were always in the way when you wanted to get anywhere in a hurry.

"An' you are in a 'urry w'en you sees a Minnie [Minnenwerfer] comin' your w'y. But you gets trench legs arter a w'ile. It'll be a funny sight to see blokes walkin' along the street in Lunnon w'en the war's over. They'll be so used to dodgin' in an' out o' traverses they won't be able to go in a straight line."

As we walked through the firing-line trenches, I could quite understand the possibility of one's acquiring trench legs. Five paces forward, two to the right, two to the left, two to the left again, then five to the right, and so on to Switzerland. Shorty was of the opinion that one could enter the trenches on the Channel coast and walk through to the Alps without once coming out on top of the ground. I am not in a position either to affirm or to question this statement. My own experience was confined to that part of the British front which lies between Messines in Belgium and Loos in France. There, certainly, one could walk for miles, through an intricate maze of continuous underground passages.

But the firing-line trench was neither a traffic route nor a promenade. The great bulk of inter-trench business passed through the traveling trench, about fifteen yards in rear of the fire trench and running parallel to it. The two were connected by many passageways, the chief difference between them being that the fire trench was the business district, while the traveling trench was primarily residential. Along the latter were built most of the dugouts, lavatories, and trench kitchens. The sleeping quarters for the men were not very elaborate. Recesses were made in the wall of the trench about two feet above the floor. They were not more than three feet high, so that one had to crawl in head first when going to bed. They were partitioned in the middle, and were supposed to offer accommodation for four men, two on each side. But, as Shorty said, everything depended on the ration allowance. Two men who had eaten to repletion could not hope to occupy the same apartment. One had a choice of going to bed hungry or of eating heartily and sleeping outside on the firing-bench.

"'Ere's a funny thing," he said. "W'y do you suppose they makes the dugouts open at one end?"

I had no explanation to offer.

"Crawl inside an' I'll show you."

I stood my rifle against the side of the trench and crept in.

"Now, yer supposed to be asleep," said Shorty, and with that he gave me a whack on the soles of my boots with his entrenching tool handle. I can still feel the pain of the blow.

"Stand to! Wyke up 'ere! Stand to!" he shouted, and gave me another resounding wallop.

I backed out in all haste.

"Get the idea? That's 'ow they wykes you up at stand-to, or w'en your turn comes fer sentry. Not bad, wot?"

I said that it all depended on whether one was doing the waking or the sleeping, and that, for my part, when sleeping, I would lie with my head out.

"You wouldn't if you belonged to our lot. They'd give it to you on the napper just as quick as 'it you on the feet. You ain't on to the game, that's all. Let me show you suthin'."

He crept inside and drew his knees up to his chest so that his feet were well out of reach. At his suggestion I tried to use the active service alarm clock on him, but there was not room enough in which to wield it. My feet were tingling from the effect of his blows, and I felt that the reputation for resourcefulness of Kitchener's Mob was at stake. In a moment of inspiration I seized my rifle, gave him a dig in the shins with the butt, and shouted, "Stand to, Shorty!" He came out rubbing his leg ruefully.

"You got the idea, mate," he said. "That's just wot they does w'en you tries to double-cross 'em by pullin' yer feet in. I ain't sure w'ere I likes it best, on the shins or on the feet."

This explanation of the reason for building three-sided dugouts, while not, of course, the true one, was none the less interesting. And certainly, the task of arousing sleeping men for sentry duty was greatly facilitated with rows of protruding boot soles "simply arskin' to be 'it," as Shorty put it.

All of the dugouts for privates and N.C.O.s were of equal size and built on the same model, the reason being that the walls and floors, which were made of wood, and the roofs, which were of corrugated iron, were put together in sections at the headquarters of the Royal Engineers, who superintended all the work of trench construction. The material was brought up at night ready to be fitted into excavations.

Furthermore, with thousands of men to house within a very limited area, space was a most important consideration. There was no room for indulging individual tastes in dugout architecture. The roofs were covered with from three to four feet of earth, which made them proof against shrapnel or shell splinters. In case of a heavy bombardment with high explosives, the men took shelter in deep and narrow "slip trenches." These were blind alleyways leading off from the traveling trench, with room for from ten to fifteen men in each. At this part of the line there were none of the very deep shell-proof shelters, from fifteen to twenty feet below the surface of the ground, of which I had read. Most of the men seemed to be glad of this. They preferred taking their chances in an open trench during heavy shell fire.

Realists and Romanticists lived side by side in the traveling trench. "My Little Gray Home in the West" was the modest legend over one apartment. The "Ritz Carlton" was next door to "The Rats' Retreat," with "Vermin Villa" next door but one. "The Suicide Club" was the suburban residence of some members of the bombing squad. I remarked that the bombers seemed to take rather a pessimistic view of their profession, whereupon Shorty told me that if there were any men slated for the Order of the Wooden Cross, the bombers were those unfortunate ones. In an assault they were first at the enemy's position. They had dangerous work to do even on the quietest of days. But theirs was a post of honor, and no one of them but was proud of his membership in the Suicide Club.

The officers' quarters were on a much more generous and elaborate scale than those of the men. This I gathered from Shorty's description of them, for I saw only the exteriors as we passed along the trench. Those for platoon and company commanders were built along the traveling trench. The colonel, major, and adjutant lived in a luxurious palace, about fifty yards down a communication trench. Near it was the officers' mess, a cafe de luxe with glass panels in the door, a cooking stove, a long wooden table, chairs,--everything, in fact, but hot and cold running water.

"You know," said Shorty, "the officers thinks they 'as to rough it, but they got it soft, I'm tellin' you! Wooden bunks to sleep in, batmen to bring 'em 'ot water fer shavin' in the mornin', all the fags they wants,--Blimy, I wonder wot they calls livin' 'igh?"

I agreed that in so far as living quarters are concerned, they were roughing it under very pleasant circumstances. However, they were not always so fortunate, as later experience proved. Here there had been little serious fighting for months and the trenches were at their best. Elsewhere the officers' dugouts were often but little better than those of the men.

The first-line trenches were connected with two lines of support or reserve trenches built in precisely the same fashion, and each heavily wired. The communication trenches which joined them were from seven to eight feet deep and wide enough to permit the convenient passage of incoming and outgoing troops, and the transport of the wounded back to the field dressing stations. From the last reserve line they wound on backward through the fields until troops might leave them well out of range of rifle fire. Under Shorty's guidance I saw the field dressing stations, the dugouts for the reserve ammunition supply and the stores of bombs and hand grenades, battalion and brigade trench headquarters. We wandered from one part of the line to another through trenches, all of which were kept amazingly neat and clean. The walls were stayed with fine-mesh wire to hold the earth in place. The floors were covered with board walks carefully laid over the drains, which ran along the center of the trench and emptied into deep wells, built in recesses in the walls. I felt very much encouraged when I saw the careful provisions for sanitation and drainage. On a fine June morning it seemed probable that living in ditches was not to be so unpleasant as I had imagined it. Shorty listened to my comments with a smile.

"Don't pat yerself on the back yet a w'ile, mate," he said. "They looks right enough now, but wite till you've seen 'em arter a 'eavy rain."

I had this opportunity many times during the summer and autumn. A more wretched existence than that of soldiering in wet weather could hardly be imagined. The walls of the trenches caved in in great masses. The drains filled to overflowing, and the trench walks were covered deep in mud. After a few hours of rain, dry and comfortable trenches became a quagmire, and we were kept busy for days afterward repairing the damage.

As a machine gunner I was particularly interested in the construction of the machine-gun emplacements. The covered battle positions were very solidly built. The roofs were supported with immense logs or steel girders covered over with many layers of sandbags. There were two carefully concealed loopholes looking out to a flank, but none for frontal fire, as this dangerous little weapon best enjoys catching troops in enfilade owing to the rapidity and the narrow cone of its fire. Its own front is protected by the guns on its right and left. At each emplacement there was a range chart giving the ranges to all parts of the enemy's trenches, and to every prominent object both in front of and behind them, within its field of fire. When not in use the gun was kept mounted and ready for action in the battle position.

"But remember this," said Shorty, "you never fires from your battle position except in case of attack. W'en you goes out at night to 'ave a little go at Fritzie, you always tykes yer gun sommers else. If you don't, you'll 'ave Minnie an' Busy Bertha an' all the rest o' the Krupp childern comin' over to see w'ere you live."

This was a wise precaution, as we were soon to learn from experience. Machine guns are objects of special interest to the artillery, and the locality from which they are fired becomes very unhealthy for some little time thereafter.

We stopped for a moment at "The Mud Larks' Hairdressing Parlor," a very important institution if one might judge by its patronage. It was housed in a recess in the wall of the traveling trench, and was open to the sky. There I saw the latest fashion in "oversea" hair cuts. The victims sat on a ration box while the barber mowed great swaths through tangled thatch with a pair of close-cutting clippers. But instead of making a complete job of it, a thick fringe of hair which resembled a misplaced scalping tuft was left for decorative purposes, just above the forehead. The effect was so grotesque that I had to invent an excuse for laughing. It was a lame one, I fear, for Shorty looked at me warningly. When we had gone on a little way he said:--

"Ain't it a proper beauty parlor? But you got to be careful about larfin'. Some o' the blokes thinks that 'edge-row is a regular ornament."

I had supposed that a daily shave was out of the question on the firing-line; but the British Tommy is nothing if not resourceful. Although water is scarce and fuel even more so, the self-respecting soldier easily surmounts difficulties, and the Gloucesters were all nice in matters pertaining to the toilet. Instead of draining their canteens of tea, they saved a few drops for shaving purposes.

"It's a bit sticky," said Shorty, "but it's 'ot, an' not 'arf bad w'en you gets used to it. Now, another thing you don't want to ferget is this: W'en yer movin' up fer yer week in the first line, always bring a bundle o' firewood with you. They ain't so much as a match-stick left in the trenches. Then you wants to be savin' of it.

Don't go an' use it all the first d'y or you'll 'ave to do without yer tea the rest o' the week."

I remembered his emphasis upon this point afterward when I saw men risking their lives in order to procure firewood. Without his tea Tommy was a wretched being. I do not remember a day, no matter how serious the fighting, when he did not find both the time and the means for making it.

Shorty was a Ph.D. in every subject in the curriculum, including domestic science. In preparing breakfast he gave me a practical demonstration of the art of conserving a limited resource of fuel, bringing our two canteens to a boil with a very meager handful of sticks; and while doing so he delivered an oral thesis on the best methods of food preparation. For example, there was the item of corned beef--familiarly called "bully." It was the piece de resistance *at every meal with the possible exception of breakfast, when there was usually a strip of bacon. Now, one's appetite for "bully" becomes jaded in the course of a few weeks or months. To use the German expression one doesn't eat it* gern. But it is not a question of liking it. One must eat it or go hungry. Therefore, said Shorty, save carefully all of your bacon grease, and instead of eating your "bully" cold out of the tin, mix it with bread crumbs and grated cheese and fry it in the grease. He prepared some in this way, and I thought it a most delectable dish. Another way of stimulating the palate was to boil the beef in a solution of bacon grease and water, and then, while eating it, "kid yourself that it's Irish stew." This second method of taking away the curse did not appeal to me very strongly, and Shorty admitted that he practiced such self-deception with very indifferent success; for after all "bully" was "bully" in whatever form you ate it.

In addition to this staple, the daily rations consisted of bacon, bread, cheese, jam, army biscuits, tea, and sugar. Sometimes they received a tinned meat and vegetable ration, already cooked, and at welcome intervals fresh meat and potatoes were substituted for corned beef. Each man had a very generous allowance of food, a great deal more, I thought, than he could possibly eat. Shorty explained this by saying that allowance was made for the amount which would be consumed by the rats and the blue-bottle flies.

There were, in fact, millions of flies. They settled in great swarms along the walls of the trenches, which were filled to the brim with warm light as soon as the sun had climbed a little way up the sky. Empty tin-lined ammunition boxes were used as cupboards for food. But of what avail were cupboards to a jam-loving and jam-fed British army living in open ditches in the summer time? Flytraps made of empty jam tins were set along the top of the parapet. As soon as one was filled, another was set in its place. But it was an unequal war against an expeditionary force of countless numbers.

"They ain't nothin' you can do," said Shorty. "They steal the jam right off yer bread."

As for the rats, speaking in the light of later experience, I can say that an army corps of pied pipers would not have sufficed to entice away the hordes of them that infested the trenches, living like house pets on our rations. They were great lazy animals, almost as large as cats, and so gorged with food that they could hardly move. They ran over us in the dugouts at night, and filched cheese and crackers right through the heavy waterproofed covering of our haversacks. They squealed and fought among themselves at all hours. I think it possible that they were carrion eaters, but never, to my knowledge, did they attack living men. While they were unpleasant bedfellows, we became so accustomed to them that we were not greatly concerned about our very intimate associations.

Our course of instruction at the Parapet-etic School was brought to a close late in the evening when we shouldered our packs, bade good-bye to our friends the Gloucesters, and marched back in the moonlight to our billets. I had gained an entirely new conception of trench life, of the difficulties involved in trench building, and the immense amount of material and labor needed for the work.

Americans who are interested in learning of these things at first hand will do well to make the grand tour of the trenches when the war is finished. Perhaps the thrifty continentals will seek to commercialize such advantage as misfortune has brought them, in providing favorable opportunities. Perhaps the Touring Club of France will lay out a new route, following the windings of the firing line from the Channel coast across the level fields of Flanders, over the Vosges Mountains to the borders of Switzerland. Pedestrians may wish to make the journey on foot, cooking their supper over Tommy's rusty biscuit-tin stoves, sleeping at night in the dugouts where he lay shivering with cold during the winter nights of 1914 and 1915. If there are enthusiasts who will be satisfied with only the most intimate personal view of the trenches, if there are those who would try to understand the hardships and discomforts of trench life by living it during a summer vacation, I would suggest that they remember Private Shorty Holloway's parting injunction to me:--

"Now, don't ferget, Jamie!" he said as we shook hands, "always 'ave a box o' Keatings 'andy, an' 'ang on to yer extra shirt!"

CHAPTER VII
MIDSUMMER CALM

During our first summer in the trenches there were days, sometimes weeks at a time, when, in the language of the official bulletins, there was "nothing to report," or "calm" prevailed "along our entire front." From the War Office point of view these statements were, doubtless, true enough. But from Tommy Atkins's point of view, "calm" was putting it somewhat mildly. Life in the trenches, even on the quietest of days, is full of adventure highly spiced with danger. Snipers, machine gunners, artillerymen, airmen, engineers of the opposing sides, vie with each other in skill and daring, in order to secure that coveted advantage, the morale. Tommy calls it the "more-ale," but he jolly well knows when he has it and when he hasn't.

There were many nights of official calm when we machine gunners crept out of the trenches with our guns to positions prepared beforehand, either in front of the line or to the rear of it. There we waited for messages from our listening patrols, who were lying in the tall grass of "the front yard." They sent word to us immediately when they discovered enemy working parties building up their parapets or mending their barbed-wire entanglements. We would then lay our guns according to instructions received and blaze away, each gun firing at the rate of from three hundred to five hundred rounds per minute. After a heavy burst of fire, we would change our positions at once. It was then that the most exciting part of our work began. For as soon as we ceased firing, there were answering fusillades from hundreds of German rifles. And within two or three minutes, German field artillery began a search for us with shrapnel. We crawled from one position to another over the open ground or along shallow ditches, dug for the purpose. These offered protection from rifle fire, but frequently the shell fire was so heavy and so well directed that we were given some very unpleasant half-hours, lying flat on our faces, listening to the deafening explosions and the vicious whistling of flying shrapnel.

We fired from the trenches, as well as in front and to the rear of them. We were, in fact, busy during most of the night, for it was our duty to see to it that our guns lived up to their reputation as "weapons of opportunity and surprise." With the aid of large-scale maps, we located all of the roads, within range, back of the German lines; roads which we knew were used by enemy troops moving in and out of the trenches. We located all of their communication trenches leading back to the rear; and at uncertain intervals we covered roads and trenches with bursts of searching fire.

The German gunners were by no means inactive. They, too, profited by their knowledge of night life in the firing-line, their knowledge of soldier nature. They knew, as did we, that the roads in the rear of the trenches are filled, at night, with troops, transport wagons, and fatigue parties. They knew, as did we, that men become so utterly weary of living in ditches--living in holes, like rats--that they are willing to take big risks when moving in or out of the trenches, for the pure joy of getting up on top of the ground. Many a night when we were moving up for our week in the first line, or back for our week in reserve, we heard the far-off rattle of German Maxims, and in an instant, the bullets would be zip-zipping all around us. There was no need for the sharp word of command. If there was a communication trench at hand, we all made a dive for it at once. If there was not, we fell face down, in ditches, shell holes, in any place which offered a little protection from that terrible hail of lead. Many of our men were killed and wounded nightly by machine-gun fire, usually because they were too tired to be cautious. And, doubtless, we did as much damage with our own guns. It seemed to me horrible, something in the nature of murder, that advantage must be taken of these opportunities. But it was all a part of the game of war; and fortunately, we rarely knew, nor did the Germans, what damage was done during those summer nights of "calm along the entire front."

The artillerymen, both British and German, did much to relieve the boredom of those "nothing to report" days. There were desultory bombardments of the trenches at daybreak, and at dusk, when every infantryman is at his post, rifle in hand, bayonet fixed, on the alert for signs of a surprise attack. If it was a bombardment with shrapnel, Tommy was not greatly concerned, for in trenches he is fairly safe from shrapnel fire. But if the shells were large-caliber high explosives, he crouched close to the front wall of the trench, lamenting the day he was foolish enough to become an infantryman, "a bloomin' 'uman ninepin!" Covered with dirt, sometimes half-buried in fallen trench, he wagered his next week's tobacco rations that the London papers would print the same old story: "Along the western front there is nothing to report." And usually he won.

Trench mortaring was more to our liking. That is an infantryman's game, and, while extremely hazardous, the men in the trenches have a sporting chance. Every one forgot breakfast when word was passed down the line that we were going to "mortarfy" Fritzie. The last-relief night sentries, who had just tumbled sleepily into their dugouts, tumbled out of them again to watch the fun. Fatigue parties, working in the communication trenches, dropped their picks and shovels and came hurrying up to the first line. Eagerly, expectantly, every one waited for the sport to begin. Our projectiles were immense balls of hollow steel, filled with high explosive of tremendous power. They were fired from a small gun, placed, usually, in the first line of reserve trenches. A dull boom from the rear warned us that the game had started.

"There she is!" "See 'er? Goin' true as a die!" "She's go'n' to 'it! She's go'n' to 'it!" All of the boys would be shouting at once. Up it goes, turning over and over, rising to a height of several hundred feet. Then, if well aimed, it reaches the end of its upward journey directly over the enemy's line, and falls straight into his trench. There is a moment of silence, followed by a terrific explosion which throws dirt and debris high in the air. By this time every Tommy along the line is standing on the firing-bench, head and shoulders above the parapet, quite forgetting his own danger in his excitement, and shouting at the top of his voice.

"'Ow's that one, Fritzie boy?"

"Gooten morgen, you Proosian sausage-wallopers!"

"Tyke a bit o' that there 'ome to yer missus!"

But Fritzie could be depended upon to keep up his end of the game. He gave us just as good as we sent, and often he added something for full measure. His surprises were sausage-shaped missiles which came wobbling toward us, slowly, almost awkwardly; but they dropped with lightning speed, and alas, for any poor Tommy who misjudged the place of its fall! However, every one had a chance. Trench-mortar projectiles are so large that one can see them coming, and they describe so leisurely an arc before they fall that men have time to run.

I have always admired Tommy Atkins for his sense of fair play. He enjoyed giving Fritz "a little bit of all-right," but he never resented it when Fritz had his own fun at our expense. In the far-off days of peace, I used to lament the fact that we had fallen upon evil times. I read of old wars with a feeling of regret that men had lost their old primal love for dangerous sport, their naive ignorance of fear. All the brave, heroic things of life were said and done. But on those trench-mortaring days, when I watched boys playing with death with right good zest, heard them shouting and laughing as they tumbled over one another in their eagerness to escape it, I was convinced of my error. Daily I saw men going through the test of fire triumphantly, and, at the last, what a severe test it was! And how splendidly they met it! During six months continuously in the firing-line, I met less than a dozen natural-born cowards; and my experience was largely with plumbers, drapers' assistants, clerks, men who had no fighting traditions to back them up, make them heroic in spite of themselves.

The better I knew Tommy, the better I liked him. He hasn't a shred of sentimentality in his make-up. There is plenty of sentiment, sincere feeling, but it is admirably concealed. I had been a soldier of the King for many months before I realized that the men with whom I was living, sharing rations and hardships, were anything other than the healthy animals they looked. They relished their food and talked about it. They grumbled at the restraints military discipline imposed upon them, and at the paltry shilling a day which they received for the first really hard work they had ever done. They appeared to regard England as a miserly employer, exacting their last ounce of energy for a wretchedly inadequate wage. To the casual observer, theirs was not the ardor of loyal sons, fighting for a beloved motherland. Rather, it seemed that of irresponsible schoolboys on a long holiday. They said nothing about patriotism or the duty of Englishmen in war-time. And if I attempted to start a conversation along that line, they walked right over me with their boots on.

This was a great disappointment at first. I should never have known, from anything that was said, that a man of them was stirred at the thought of fighting for old

England. England was all right, but "I ain't goin' balmy about the old flag and all that stuff." Many of them insisted that they were in the army for personal and selfish reasons alone. They went out of their way to ridicule any and every indication of sentiment.

There was the matter of talk about mothers, for example. I can't imagine this being the case in a volunteer army of American boys, but not once, during fifteen months of British army life, did I hear a discussion of mothers. When the weekly parcels from England arrived and the boys were sharing their cake and chocolate and tobacco, one of them would say, "Good old mum. She ain't a bad sort"; to be answered with reluctant, mouth-filled grunts, or grudging nods of approval. As for fathers, I often thought to myself, "What a tremendous army of posthumous sons!" Months before I would have been astonished at this reticence. But I had learned to understand Tommy. His silences were as eloquent as any splendid outbursts or glowing tributes could have been. Indeed, they were far more eloquent! Englishmen seem to have an instinctive understanding of the futility, the emptiness, of words in the face of unspeakable experiences. It was a matter of constant wonder to me that men, living in the daily and hourly presence of death, could so surely control and conceal their feelings. Their talk was of anything but home; and yet, I knew they thought of but little else.

One of our boys was killed, and there was the letter to be written to his parents. Three Tommies who knew him best were to attempt this. They made innumerable beginnings. Each of them was afraid of blundering, of causing unnecessary pain by an indelicate revelation of the facts. There was a feminine fineness about their concern which was beautiful to see. The final draft of the letter was a little masterpiece, not of English, but of insight; such a letter as any one of us would have wished his own parents to receive under like circumstances. Nothing was forgotten which could have made the news in the slightest degree more endurable. Every trifling personal belonging was carefully saved and packed in a little box to follow the letter. All of this was done amid much boisterous jesting. And there was the usual hilarious singing to the wheezing accompaniment of an old mouth-organ. But of reference to home, or mothers, or comradeship,--nothing.

Rarely a night passed without its burial parties. "Digging in the garden" Tommy calls the grave-making. The bodies, wrapped in blankets or waterproof ground-sheets, are lifted over the parados, and carried back a convenient twenty yards or more. The desolation of that garden, choked with weeds and a wild growth of self-sown crops, is indescribable. It was wreckage-strewn, gaping with shell holes, billowing with innumerable graves, a waste land speechlessly pathetic. The poplar trees and willow hedges have been blasted and splintered by shell fire. Tommy calls these "Kaiser Bill's flowers." Coming from England, he feels more deeply than he would care to admit the crimes done to trees in the name of war.

Our chaplain was a devout man, but prudent to a fault. Never, to my knowledge, did he visit us in the trenches. Therefore our burial parties proceeded without the rites of the Church. This arrangement was highly satisfactory to Tommy. He liked to "get the planting done" with the least possible delay or fuss. His whispered conversations while the graves were being scooped were, to say the least, quite out of the spirit of the occasion. Once we were burying two boys with whom we had been having supper a few hours before. There was an artillery duel in progress, the shells whistling high over our heads, and bursting in great splotches of white fire, far in rear of the opposing lines of trenches. The grave-making went speedily on, while the burial party argued in whispers as to the caliber of the guns. Some said they were six-inch, while others thought nine-inch. Discussion was momentarily suspended when a trench rocket shot in an arc from the enemy's line. We crouched, motionless, until the welcome darkness spread again.

And then, in loud whispers:--

"'Ere! If they was nine-inch, they would 'ave more screech."

And one from the other school of opinion would reply:--

"Don't talk so bloomin' silly! Ain't I a-tellin' you that you can't always size 'em by the screech?"

Not a prayer; not a word, either of censure or of praise, for the boys who had gone; not an expression of opinion as to the meaning of the great change which had come to them and which might come, as suddenly, to any or all of us. And yet I knew that they were each thinking of these things.

There were days when the front was really quiet. The thin trickle of rifle fire only accentuated the stillness of an early summer morning. Far down the line Tommy could be heard, singing to himself as he sat in the door of his dugout, cleaning his rifle, or making a careful scrutiny of his shirt for those unwelcome little parasites which made life so miserable for him at all times. There were pleasant cracklings of burning pine sticks and the sizzle of frying bacon. Great swarms of bluebottle flies buzzed lazily in the warm sunshine. Sometimes, across a pool of noonday silence, we heard birds singing; for the birds didn't desert us. When we gave them a hearing, they did their cheery little best to assure us that everything would come right in the end. Once we heard a skylark, an English skylark, singing over No-Man's-Land! I scarcely know which gave me more pleasure, the song, or the sight of the faces of those English lads as they listened. I was deeply touched when one of them said:--

"Ain't 'e a plucky little chap, singin' right in front of Fritzie's trenches fer us English blokes?"

It was a sincere and fitting tribute, as perfect for a soldier as Shelley's "Ode" for a poet.

Along the part of the British front which we held during the summer, the opposing lines of trenches were from less than a hundred to four hundred and fifty or five hundred yards apart. When we were neighborly as regards distance, we were also neighborly as regards social intercourse. In the early mornings when the heavy night mists still concealed the lines, the boys stood head and shoulders above the parapet and shouted:--

"Hi, Fritzie!"

And the greeting was returned:--

"Hi, Tommy!"

Then we conversed. Very few of us knew German, but it is surprising how many Germans could speak English. Frequently they shouted, "Got any 'woodbines,' Tommy?"--his favorite brand of cigarettes; and Tommy would reply, "Sure! Shall I bring 'em over or will you come an' fetch 'em?" This was often the ice-breaker, the beginning of a conversation which varied considerably in other details.

"Who are you?" Fritzie would shout.

And Tommy, "We're the King's Own 'Ymn of 'Aters"; some such subtle repartee as that. "Wot's your mob?"

"We're a battalion of Irish rifles." The Germans liked to provoke us by pretending that the Irish were disloyal to England.

Sometimes they shouted:--

"Any of you from London?"

"Not arf! Wot was you a-doin' of in London? Witin' tible at Sam Isaac's fish-shop?"

The rising of the mists put an end to these conversations. Sometimes they were concluded earlier with bursts of rifle and machine-gun fire. "All right to be friendly," Tommy would say, "but we got to let 'em know this ain't no love-feast."

CHAPTER VIII
UNDER COVER

I. UNSEEN FORCES

"We come acrost the Channel
For to wallop Germany;
But they 'aven't got no soldiers--
Not that any one can see.
They plug us with their rifles
An' they let their shrapnel fly,
But they never takes a pot at us
Exceptin' on the sly.

 Chorus
"Fritzie w'en you comin' out?
This wot you calls a fight?
You won't never get to Calais
Always keepin' out o' sight.

"We're a goin' back to Blightey--
Wot's the use a-witin' 'ere
Like a lot o' bloomin' mud-larks
Fer old Fritzie to appear?
'E never puts 'is napper up

> Above the parapet.
> We been in France fer seven months
> An' 'aven't seen 'im yet!"

So sang Tommy, the incorrigible parodist, during the long summer days and nights of 1915, when he was impatiently waiting for something to turn up. For three months and more we were face to face with an enemy whom we rarely saw. It was a weird experience. Rifles cracked, bullets zip-zipped along the top of the parapet, great shells whistled over our heads or tore immense holes in the trenches, trench-mortar projectiles and hand-grenades were hurled at us, and yet there was not a living soul to be seen across the narrow strip of No-Man's-Land, whence all this murderous rain of steel and lead was coming. Daily we kept careful and continuous watch, searching the long, curving line of German trenches and the ground behind them with our periscopes and field-glasses, and nearly always with the same barren result. We saw only the thin wreaths of smoke rising, morning and evening, from trench fires; the shattered trees, the forlorn and silent ruins, the long grass waving in the wind.

Although we were often within two hundred yards of thousands of German soldiers, rarely farther than four hundred yards away, I did not see one of them until we had been in the trenches for more than six weeks, and then only for the interval of a second or two. My German was building up a piece of damaged parapet. I watched the earth being thrown over the top of the trench, when suddenly a head appeared, only to be immediately withdrawn. One of our snipers had evidently been watching, too. A rifle cracked and I saw a cloud of dust arise where the bullet clipped the top of the parapet. The German waved his spade defiantly in the air and continued digging; but he remained discreetly under cover thereafter.

This marked an epoch in my experience in a war of unseen forces. I had actually beheld a German, although Tommy insisted that it was only the old caretaker, "the bloke wot keeps the trenches tidy." This mythical personage, a creature of Tommy's own fancy, assumed a very real importance during the summer when the attractions at the Western Theater of War were only mildly interesting. "Carl the caretaker" was supposed to be a methodical old man whom the Emperor had left in charge of his trenches on the western front during the absence of the German armies in Russia. Many were the stories told about him at different parts of the line. Sometimes he was endowed with a family. His "missus" and his "three little nippers" were with him, and together they were blocking the way to Berlin of the entire British Army. Sometimes he was "Hans the Grenadier," owing to his fondness for nightly bombing parties. Sometimes he was "Minnie's husband," Minnie being that redoubtable lady known in polite military circles as a "Minnenwerfer." As already explained, she was sausage-like in shape, and frightfully demonstrative. When she went visiting at the behest of her husband, Tommy usually contrived to be "not at home," whereupon Minnie wrecked the house and disappeared in a cloud of dense black smoke.

One imagines all sorts of monstrous things about an unseen enemy. The strain of constantly watching and seeing nothing became almost unbearable at times. We were often too far apart to have our early morning interchange of courtesies, and then the constant phtt-phtt of bullets annoyed and exasperated us. I for one welcomed any evidence that our opponents were fathers and husbands and brothers just as we were. I remember my delight, one fine summer morning, at seeing three great kites soaring above the German line. There is much to be said for men who enjoy flying kites. Once they mounted a dummy figure of a man on their parapet. Tommy had great sport shooting at it, the Germans jiggling its arms and legs in a most laughable manner whenever a hit was registered. In their eagerness to "get a good bead" on the figure, the men threw caution to the winds, and stood on the firing-benches, shooting over the top of the parapet. Fritz and Hans were true sportsmen while the fun was on, and did not once fire at us. Then the dummy was taken down, and we returned to the more serious game of war with the old deadly earnestness. I recall such incidents with joy as I remember certain happy events in childhood. We needed these trivial occurrences to keep us sane and human. There were not many of them, but such as there were, we talked of for days and weeks afterward.

As for the matter of keeping out of sight, there was a good deal to be said on both sides. Although Tommy was impatient with his prudent enemy and sang songs, twitting him about always keeping under cover, he did not usually forget, in the daytime at least, to make his own observations of the German line with caution. Telescopic sights have made the business of sniping an exact science. They magnify the object aimed at many diameters, and if it remains in view long enough to permit the pulling of a trigger, the chances of a hit are almost one hundred per cent.

II. "THE BUTT-NOTCHER"

Snipers have a roving commission. They move from one part of the line to another, sometimes firing from carefully concealed loopholes in the parapet, sometimes from snipers' nests in trees or hedges. Often they creep out into the tall grass of No-Man's-Land. There, with a plentiful supply of food and ammunition, they remain for a day or two at a time, lying in wait for victims. It was a cold-blooded business, and hateful to some of the men. With others, the passion for it grew. They kept tally of their victims by cutting notches on the butts of their rifles.

I well remember the pleasant June day when I first met a "butt-notcher." I was going for water, to an old farmhouse about half a mile from our sector of trench. It was a day of bright sunshine. Poppies and buttercups had taken root in the banks of earth heaped up on either side of the communication trench. They were nodding their heads as gayly in the breeze as of old did Wordsworth's daffodils in the quiet countryside at Rydal Mount. It was a joy to see them there, reminding one that God was still in his heaven, whatever might be wrong with the world. It was a joy to be alive, a joy which one could share unselfishly with friend and enemy alike. The colossal stupidity of war was never more apparent to me than upon that day. I hated my job, and if I hated any man, it was the one who had invented the murderous little weapon known as a machine gun.

I longed to get out on top of the ground. I wanted to lie at full length in the grass; for it was June, and Nature has a way of making one feel the call of June, even from the bottom of a communication trench seven feet deep. Flowers and grass peep down at one, and white clouds sail placidly across

"The strip of blue we prisoners call the sky."

I felt that I must see all of the sky and see it at once. Therefore I set down my water-cans, one on top of the other, stepped up on them, and was soon over the top of the trench, crawling through the tall grass toward a clump of willows about fifty yards away. I passed two lonely graves with their wooden crosses hidden in depths of shimmering, waving green, and found an old rifle, its stock weather-warped and the barrel eaten away with rust. The ground was covered with tin cans, fragments of shell-casing, and rubbish of all sorts; but it was hidden from view. Men had been laying waste the earth during the long winter, and now June was healing the wounds with flowers and cool green grasses.

I was sorry that I went to the willows, for it was there that I found the sniper. He had a wonderfully concealed position, which was made bullet-proof with steel plates and sandbags, all covered so naturally with growing grass and willow bushes that it would have been impossible to detect it at a distance of ten yards. In fact, I would not have discovered it had it not been for the loud crack of a rifle sounding so close at hand. I crept on to investigate and found the sniper looking quite disappointed.

"Missed the blighter!" he said. Then he told me that it wasn't a good place for a sniper's nest at all. For one thing, it was too far back, nearly a half-mile from the German trenches. Furthermore, it was a mistake to plant a nest in a solitary clump of willows such as this: a clump of trees offers too good an aiming mark for artillery: much better to make a position right out in the open. However, so far he had not been annoyed by shell fire. A machine gun had searched for him, but he had adequate cover from machine-gun fire.

"But, blimy! You ought to 'a' 'eard the row w'en the bullets was a-smackin' against the sandbags! Somebody was a-knockin' at the door, I give you my word!"

However, it wasn't such a "dusty little coop," and he had a good field of fire. He had registered four hits during the day, and he proudly displayed four new notches on a badly notched butt in proof of the fact.

"There's a big 'ole w'ere the artill'ry pushed in their parapet larst night. That's w'ere I caught me larst one, 'bout a 'arf-hour ago. A bloke goes by every little w'ile an' fergets to duck 'is napper. Tyke yer field-glasses an' watch me clip the next one. Quarter left it is, this side the old 'ouse with the 'ole in the wall."

I focused my glasses and waited. Presently he said, in a very cool, matter-of-fact voice:--

"There's one comin'. See 'im? 'E's carryin' a plank. You can see it stickin' up above the parapet. 'E's a-go'n' to get a nasty one if 'e don't duck w'en he comes to that 'ole."

I found the moving plank and followed it along the trench as it approached nearer and nearer to the opening; and I was guilty of the most unprofessional conduct, for I kept thinking, as hard as I could, "Duck, Fritzie! Whatever you do, duck when you come to that hole!" And surely enough, he did. The plank was lowered into the trench just before the opening was reached, and the top of it reappeared again, a moment later, on the other side of the opening. The sniper was greatly disappointed.

"Now, wouldn't that give you the camel's 'ump?" he said. "I believe you're a Joner to me, matey."

Presently another man carrying a plank went along the trench and he ducked, too.

"Grease off, Jerry!" said the butt-notcher. "Yer bringin' me bad luck. 'Owever, they prob'ly got that place taped. They lost one man there an' they won't lose another, not if they knows it."

I talked with many snipers at different parts of the line. It was interesting to get their points of view, to learn what their reaction was to their work. The butt-notchers were very few. Although snipers invariably took pride in their work, it was the sportsman's pride in good marksmanship rather than the love of killing for its own sake. The general attitude was that of a corporal whom I knew. He never fired hastily, but when he did pull the trigger, his bullet went true to the mark.

"You can't 'elp feelin' sorry for the poor blighters," he would say, "but it's us or them, an' every one you knocks over means one of our blokes saved."

I have no doubt that the Germans felt the same way about us. At any rate, they thoroughly believed in the policy of attrition, and in carrying it out they often wasted thousands of rounds in sniping every yard of our parapet. The sound was deafening at times, particularly when there were ruined walls of houses or a row of trees just back of our trenches. The ear-splitting reports were hurled against them and seemed to be shattered into thousands of fragments, the sound rattling and tumbling on until it died away far in the distance.

III. NIGHT ROUTINE

Meanwhile, like furtive inhabitants of an infamous underworld, we remained hidden in our lairs in the daytime, waiting for night when we could creep out of our holes and go about our business under cover of darkness. Sleep is a luxury indulged in but rarely in the first-line trenches. When not on sentry duty at night, the men were organized into working parties, and sent out in front of the trenches to mend the barbed-wire entanglements which are being constantly destroyed by artillery fire; or, in summer, to cut the tall grass and the weeds which would otherwise offer concealment to enemy listening patrols or bombing parties. Ration fatigues of twenty or thirty men per company went back to meet the battalion transport wagons at some point several miles in rear of the firing-line. There were trench supplies and stores to be brought up as well, and the never-finished business of mending and improving the trenches kept many off-duty men employed during the hours of darkness. The men on duty in front of the trenches were always in very great danger. They worked swiftly and silently, but they were often discovered, in which case the only warning they received was a sudden burst of machine-gun fire. Then would come urgent calls for "Stretcher bearers!" and soon the wreckage was brought in over the parapet. The stretchers were set down in the bottom of the trench and hasty examinations made by the light of a flash lamp.

"W'ere's 'e caught it?"

"'Ere it is, through the leg. Tyke 'is puttee off, one of you!"

"Easy, now! It's smashed the bone! Stick it, matey! We'll soon 'ave you as right as rain!"

"Fer Gawd's sake, boys, go easy! It's givin' me 'ell! Let up! Let up just a minute!"

Many a conversation of this sort did we hear at night when the field-dressings were being put on. But even in his suffering Tommy never forgot to be unrighteously indignant if he had been wounded when on a working party. What could he say to the women of England who would bring him fruit and flowers in hospital, call him a "poor brave fellow," and ask how he was wounded? He had enlisted as a soldier, and as a reward for his patriotism the Government had given him a shovel, "an' 'ere I am, workin' like a bloomin' navvy, fillin' sandbags full o' France, w'en I up an' gets plugged!" The men who most bitterly resented the pick-and-shovel phase of army life were given a great deal of it to do for that very reason. One of my comrades was shot in the leg while digging a refuse pit. The wound was a bad one and he suffered much pain, but the humiliation was even harder to bear. What could he tell them at home?

"Do you think I'm a go'n' to s'y I was a-carryin' a sandbag full of old jam tins back to the refuse pit w'en Fritzie gave me this 'ere one in the leg? Not so bloomin' likely! I was afraid I'd get one like this! Ain't it a rotten bit o' luck!"

If he had to be a casualty Tommy wanted to be an interesting one. He wanted to fall in the heat of battle, not in the heat of inglorious fatigue duty.

But there was more heroic work to be done: going out on listening patrol, for example. One patrol, consisting of a sergeant or a corporal and four or five privates, was sent out from each company. It was the duty of these men to cover the area immediately in front of the company line of trench, to see and hear without being discovered, and to report immediately any activity of the enemy, above or below ground, of which they might learn. They were on duty for from three to five hours, and might use a wide discretion in their prowlings, provided they kept within the limits of frontage allotted to their own company, and returned to the meeting-place where the change of reliefs was made. These requirements were not easily complied with, unless there were trees or other prominent landmarks standing out against the sky by means of which a patrol could keep its direction.

The work required, above everything else, cool heads and stout hearts. There was the ever-present danger of meeting an enemy patrol or bombing party, in which case, if they could not be avoided, there would be a hand-to-hand encounter with bayonets, or a noisy exchange of hand-grenades. There was danger, too, of a false alarm started by a nervous sentry. It needs but a moment for such an alarm to become general, so great is the nervous tension at which men live on the firing-line. Terrific fusillades from both sides followed while the listening patrols flattened themselves out on the ground, and listened, in no pleasant frame of mind, to the bullets whistling over their heads. But at night, and under the stress of great excitement, men fire high. Strange as it may seem, one is comparatively safe even in the open, when lying flat on the ground.

Bombing affairs were of almost nightly occurrence. Tommy enjoyed these extremely hazardous adventures which he called "Carryin' a 'app'orth o' 'ate to Fritzie," a halfpenny worth of hate, consisting of six or a dozen hand-grenades which he hurled into the German trenches from the far side of their entanglements. The more hardy spirits often worked their way through the barbed wire and, from a position close under the parapet, they waited for the sound of voices. When they had located the position of the sentries, they tossed their bombs over with deadly effect. The sound of the explosions called forth an immediate and heavy fire from sentries near and far; but lying close under the very muzzles of the German rifles, the bombers were in no danger unless a party were sent out in search of them. This, of course, constituted the chief element of risk. The strain of waiting for developments was a severe one. I have seen men come in from a "bombing stunt" worn out and trembling from nervous fatigue. And yet many of them enjoyed it, and were sent out night after night. The excitement of the thing worked into their blood.

* * * * * *

Throughout the summer there was a great deal more digging to do than fighting, for it was not until the arrival on active service of Kitchener's armies that the construction of the double line of reserve or support trenches was undertaken. From June until September this work was pushed rapidly forward. There were also trenches to be made in advance of the original firing-line, for the purpose of connecting up advanced points and removing dangerous salients. At such times there was no loafing until we had reached a depth sufficient to protect us both from view and from fire. We picked and shoveled with might and main, working in absolute silence, throwing ourselves flat on the ground whenever a trench rocket was sent up from the German lines. Casualties were frequent, but this was inevitable, working, as we did, in the open, exposed to every chance shot of an enemy sentry. The stretcher-bearers lay in the tall grass close at hand awaiting the whispered word, "Stretcher-bearers this way!" and they were kept busy during much of the time we were at work, carrying the wounded to the rear.

It was surprising how quickly the men became accustomed to the nerve-trying duties in the firing-line. Fortunately for Tommy, the longer he is in the army, the greater becomes his indifference to danger. His philosophy is fatalistic. "What is to be will be" is his only comment when one of his comrades is killed. A bullet or a shell works with such lightning speed that danger is passed before one realizes that it is at hand. Therefore, men work doggedly, carelessly, and in the background of consciousness there is always that comforting belief, common to all soldiers, that "others may be killed, but somehow, I shall escape."

The most important in-trench duty, as well as the most wearisome one for the men, is their period on "sentry-go." Eight hours in twenty-four--four two-hour shifts--each man stands at his post on the firing-bench, rifle in hand, keeping a sharp lookout over the "front yard." At night he observes as well as he can over the top of the parapet; in the daytime by means of his periscope. Most of our large periscopes were shattered by keen-sighted German snipers. We used a very good substitute, one of the simplest kind, a piece of broken pocket mirror placed on the end of a split stick, and set at an angle on top of the parados. During the two hours of sentry duty we had nothing to do other than to keep watch and keep awake. The latter was by far the more difficult business at night.

"'Ere, sergeant!" Tommy would say, as the platoon sergeant felt his way along the trench in the darkness, "w'en is the next relief comin' on? Yer watch needs a good blacksmith. I been on sentry three hours if I been a minute!"

"Never you mind about my watch, son! You got another forty-five minutes to do."

"Will you listen to that, you blokes! S'y! I could myke a better timepiece out of an old bully tin! I'm tellin' you straight, I'll be asleep w'en you come 'round again!"

But he isn't. Although the temptation may be great, Tommy isn't longing for a court-martial. When the platoon officer or the company commander makes his hourly rounds, flashing his electric pocket lamp before him, he is ready with a cheery "Post all correct, sir!" He whistles or sings to himself until, at last, he hears the platoon sergeant waking the next relief by whacking the soles of their boots with his rifle butt.

"Wake up 'ere! Come along, my lads! Your sentry-go!"

CHAPTER IX
BILLETS

Cave life had its alleviations, and chief among these was the pleasure of anticipating our week in reserve. We could look forward to this with certainty. During the long stalemate on the western front, British military organization has been perfected until, in times of quiet, it works with the monotonous smoothness of a machine. (Even during periods of prolonged and heavy fighting there is but little confusion. Only twice, during six months of campaigning, did we fail to receive our daily post of letters and parcels from England, and then, we were told, the delay was due to mine-sweeping in the Channel.) With every detail of military routine carefully thought out and every possible emergency provided for in advance, we lived as methodically in the firing-line as we had during our months of training in England.

The movements of troops in and out of the trenches were excellently arranged and timed. The outgoing battalion was prepared to move back as soon as the "relief" had taken place. The trench water-cans had been filled,--an act of courtesy between battalions,--the dugouts thoroughly cleaned, and the refuse buried. The process of "taking over" was a very brief one. The sentries of the incoming battalion were posted, and listening patrols sent out to relieve those of the outgoing battalion, which then moved down the communication trenches, the men happy in the prospect of a night of undisturbed sleep.

Second only to sleep in importance was the fortnightly bath. Sometimes we cleansed ourselves, as best we could, in muddy little duck ponds, populous with frogs and green with scum; but oh, the joy when our march ended at a military bathhouse! The Government had provided these whenever possible, and for several weeks we were within marching distance of one. There we received a fresh change of underclothing, and our uniforms were fumigated while we splashed and scrubbed in great vats of clean warm water. The order, "Everybody out!" was obeyed with great reluctance, and usually not until the bath attendants of the Army Service Corps enforced it with the cold-water hose. Tommy, who has a song for every important ceremonial, never sang, "Rule Britannia" with the enthusiasm which marked his rendition of the following chorus:--

"Whi--ter than the whitewash on the wall!   Whi--ter than the whitewash on the wall!   If yer leadin' us to slaughter   Let us 'ave our soap an' water--FIRST! Then we'll be whiter than the whitewash on the wall!"

When out of the firing-line we washed and mended our clothing and scraped a week's accumulation of mud from our uniforms. Before breakfast we were inflicted with the old punishment, Swedish drill. "Gott strafe Sweden!" Tommy would say as he puffed and perspired under a hot August sun, but he was really glad that he had no choice but to submit. In the trenches there was little opportunity for vigorous exercise, and our arms and legs became stiff with the long inactivity. Throughout the mornings we were busy with a multitude of duties. Arms and equipment were cleaned and inspected, machine guns thoroughly overhauled, gas helmets sprayed; and there was frequent instruction in bomb-throwing and bayonet-fighting in preparation for the day to which every soldier looks forward with some misgiving, but with increasing confidence--the day when the enemy shall be driven out of France.

Classes in grenade-fighting were under the supervision of officers of the Royal Engineers. In the early days of the war there was but one grenade in use, and that a crude affair made by the soldiers themselves. An empty jam tin was filled with explosive and scrap iron, and tightly bound with wire. A fuse was attached and the bomb was ready for use. But England early anticipated the importance which grenade-fighting was to play in trench warfare. Her experts in explosives were set to work, and by the time we were ready for active service, ten or a dozen varieties of bombs were in use, all of them made in the munition factories in England. The "hairbrush," the "lemon bomb," the "cricket ball," and the "policeman's truncheon" were the most important of these, all of them so-called because of their resemblance to the articles for which they were named. The first three were exploded by a time-fuse set for from three to five seconds. The fourth was a percussion bomb, which had long cloth streamers fastened to the handle to insure greater accuracy in throwing. The men became remarkably accurate at a distance of thirty to forty yards. Old cricketers were especially good, for the bomb must be thrown overhand, with a full-arm movement.

Instruction in bayonet-fighting was made as realistic as possible. Upon a given signal, we rushed forward, jumping in and out of successive lines of trenches, where dummy figures--clad in the uniforms of German foot soldiers, to give zest to the game--took our blades both front and rear with conciliatory indifference.

In the afternoon Tommy's time was his own. He could sleep, or wander along the country roads,--within a prescribed area,--or, which was more often the case, indulge in those games of chance which were as the breath of life to him. Pay-day was the event of the week in billets because it gave him the wherewithal to satisfy the promptings of his sporting blood. Our fortnightly allowance of from five to ten francs was not a princely sum; but in pennies and halfpennies, it was quite enough to provide many hours of absorbing amusement. Tommy gambled because he could not help it. When he had no money he wagered his allowance of cigarettes or his share of the daily jam ration. I believe that the appeal which war made to him was largely one to his sporting instincts. Life and Death were playing stakes for his soul with the betting odds about even.

The most interesting feature of our life in billets was the contact which it gave us with the civilian population who remained in the war zone, either because they had no place else to go, or because of that indomitable, unconquerable spirit which is characteristic of the French. There are few British soldiers along the western front who do not have memories of the heroic mothers who clung to their ruined homes as long as there was a wall standing. It was one of these who summed up for me, in five words, all the heart-breaking tragedy of war.

She kept a little shop, in Armentieres, on one of the streets leading to the firing-line. We often stopped there, when going up to the trenches, to buy loaves of delicious French bread. She had candles for sale as well, and chocolate, and packets of stationery. Her stock was exhausted daily, and in some way replenished daily. I think she made long journeys to the other side of the town, bringing back fresh supplies in a pushcart which stood outside her door. Her cottage, which was less than a mile from our first-line trenches, was partly in ruins. I couldn't understand her being there in such danger. Evidently it was with the consent of the military authorities. There were other women living on the same street; but somehow, she was different from the others. There was a spiritual fineness about her which impressed one at once. Her eyes were dry as though the tears had been drained from them, to the last drop, long ago.

One day, calling for a packet of candles, I found her standing at the barricaded window which looks toward the trenches, and the desolate towns and villages back of the German lines. My curiosity got the better of my courtesy, and I asked her, in my poor French, why she was living there. She was silent for a moment, and then she pointed toward that part of France which was on the other side of the world to us.

"Monsieur! Mes enfants! La-bas!"

Her children were over there, or had been at the outbreak of the war. That is all that she told me of her story, and I would have been a beast to have asked more. In some way she had become separated from them, and for nearly a year she had been watching there, not knowing whether her little family was living or dead.

To many of the soldiers she was just a plain, thrifty little Frenchwoman who knew not the meaning of fear, willing to risk her life daily, that she might put by something for the long hard years which would follow the war. To me she is the Spirit of France, splendid, superb France. But more than this she is the Spirit of Mother-love which wars can never alter.

Strangely enough, I had not thought of the firing-line as a boundary, a limit, during all those weeks of trench warfare. Henceforth it had a new meaning for me. I realized how completely it cut Europe in half, separating friends and relatives as thousands of miles of ocean could not have done. Roads crossed from one side to the other, but they were barricaded with sandbags and barbed-wire entanglements. At night they were deluged with shrapnel and the cobblestones were chipped and scarred with machine-gun bullets.

Tommy had a ready sympathy for the women and children who lived near the trenches. I remember many incidents which illustrate abundantly his quick understanding of the hardship and danger of their lives. Once, at Armentieres, we were marching to the baths, when the German artillery were shelling the town in the usual hit-or-miss fashion. The enemy knew, of course, that many of our troops in reserve were billeted there, and they searched for them daily. Doubtless they would have destroyed the town long ago had it not been for the fact that Lille, one of their own most important bases, is within such easy range of our batteries. As it was, they bombarded it as heavily as they dared, and on this particular morning, they were sending them over too frequently for comfort.

Some of the shells were exploding close to our line of march, but the boys tramped along with that nonchalant air which they assume in times of danger. One immense shell struck an empty house less than a block away and sent the masonry flying in every direction. The cloud of brick dust shone like gold in the sun. A moment later, a fleshy peasant woman, wearing wooden shoes, turned out of an adjoining street and ran awkwardly toward the scene of the explosion. Her movements were so clumsy and slow, in proportion to the great exertion she was making, that at any other time the sight would have been ludicrous. Now it was inevitable that such a sight should first appeal to Tommy's sense of humor, and thoughtlessly the boys started laughing and shouting at her.

"Go it, old dear! Yer makin' a grand race!"

"Two to one on Liza!"

"The other w'y, ma! That's the wrong direction! Yer runnin' right into 'em!"

She gave no heed, and a moment later we saw her gather up a little girl from a doorstep, hugging and comforting her, and shielding her with her body, instinctively, at the sound of another exploding shell. The laughter in the ranks stopped as though every man had been suddenly struck dumb.

They were courageous, those women in the firing-line. Their thoughts were always for their husbands and sons and brothers who were fighting side by side with us. Meanwhile, they kept their little shops and estaminets open for the soldiers' trade and made a brave show of living in the old way. In Armentieres a few old men lent their aid in keeping up the pretense, but the feeble little trickle of civilian life made scarcely an impression in the broad current of military activity. A solitary postman, with a mere handful of letters, made his morning rounds of echoing streets, and a bent old man with newspapers hobbled slowly along the Rue Sadi-Carnot shouting, "Le Matin! Le Journal!" to boarded windows and bolted doors. Meanwhile, we marched back and forth between billets in the town and trenches just outside. And the last thing which we saw upon leaving the town, and the first upon returning, was the lengthening row of new-made graves close to a sunny wall in the garden of the ruined convent. It was a pathetic little burial plot, filled with the bodies of women and children who had been killed in German bombardments of the town.

And thus for more than three months, while we were waiting for Fritzie to "come out," we adapted ourselves to the changing conditions of trench life and trench warfare, with a readiness which surprised and gratified us. Our very practical training in England had prepared us, in a measure, for simple and primitive living. But even with such preparation we had constantly to revise downward our standards. We lived without comforts which formerly we had regarded as absolutely essential. We lived a life so crude and rough that our army experiences in England seemed Utopian by comparison. But we throve splendidly. A government, paternalistic in its solicitude for our welfare, had schooled our bodies to withstand hardships and to endure privations. In England we had been inoculated and vaccinated whether we would or no, and the result was that fevers were practically non-existent in the trenches. What little sickness there was was due to inclement weather rather than to unsanitary conditions.

Although there were sad gaps in our ranks, the trench and camp fevers prevalent in other wars were not responsible for them. Bullets, shells, and bombs took their toll day by day, but so gradually that we had been given time to forget that we had ever known the security of civilian life. We were soon to experience the indescribable horrors of modern warfare at its worst; to be living from morning until evening and from dusk to dawn, looking upon a new day with a feeling of wonder that we had survived so long.

About the middle of September it became clear to us that the big drive was at hand. There was increased artillery activity along the entire front. The men noted with great satisfaction that the shells from our own batteries were of larger calibre. This was a welcome indication that England was at last meeting the longfelt need for high explosives.

"Lloyd George ain't been asleep," some unshaven seer would say, nodding his head wisely. "'E's a long w'ile gettin' ready, but w'en 'e is ready, there's suthin' a-go'n' to drop!"

There was a feeling of excitement everywhere. The men looked to their rifles with greater interest. They examined more carefully their bandoliers of ammunition and their gas helmets; and they were thoughtful about keeping their metal pocket mirrors and their cigarette cases in their left-hand breast pockets, for any Tommy can tell you of miraculous escapes from death due to such a protective armoring over the heart.

The thunder of guns increased with every passing day. The fire appeared to be evenly distributed over many miles of frontage. In moments of comparative quiet along our sector, we could hear them muttering and rumbling miles away to our right and left. We awaited developments with the greatest impatience, for we knew that this general bombardment was but a preliminary one for the purpose of concealing, until the last moment, the plan of attack, the portion of the front where the great artillery concentration would be made and the infantry assault pushed home. Then came sudden orders to move. Within twenty-four hours the roads were filled with the incoming troops of a new division. We made a rapid march to a rail-head, entrained, and were soon moving southward by an indirect route; southward, toward the sound of the guns, to take an inconspicuous part in the battle at Loos.

CHAPTER X
NEW LODGINGS

I. MOVING IN

We were wet and tired and cold and hungry, for we had left the train miles back of the firing-line and had been marching through the rain since early morning; but, as the sergeant said, "A bloke standin' by the side o' the road, watchin' this 'ere column pass, would think we was a-go'n' to a Sunday-school picnic." The roads were filled with endless processions of singing, shouting soldiers. Seen from a distance the long columns gave the appearance of imposing strength. One thought of them as battalions, brigades, divisions, cohesive parts of a great fighting machine. But when our lines of march crossed, when we halted to make way for each other, what an absorbing pageant of personality! Each rank was a series of intimate pictures. Everywhere there was laughing, singing, a merry minstrelsy of mouth-organs.

The jollity in my own part of the line was doubtless a picture in little of what was happening elsewhere. We were anticipating the exciting times just at hand. Mac, who was blown to pieces by a shell a few hours later, was dancing in and out of the ranks singing,--

"Oh! Won't it be joyful!   Oh! Won't it be joyful!"

Preston, who was killed at the same time, threw his rifle in the air and caught it again in sheer excess of animal spirits. Three rollicking lads, all of whom we buried during the week in the same shell hole under the same wooden cross, stumbled with an exaggerated show of utter weariness singing,--

"We never knew till now how muddy mud is,   We never knew how muddy mud could be."

And little Charley Harrison, who had fibbed bravely about his age to the recruiting officers, trudged contentedly along, his rifle slung jauntily over his shoulder, and munched army biscuit with all the relish of an old campaigner. Several days later he said good-bye to us, and made the journey back the same road, this time in a motor ambulance; and as I write, he is hobbling about a London hospital ward, one trouser leg pathetically empty.

I remember that march in the light of our later experiences, in the light of the official report of the total British casualties at Loos: sixty thousand British lads killed, wounded, and missing. Marching four abreast, a column of casualties miles in length. I see them plodding light-heartedly through the mud as they did on that gray September day, their faces wet with the rain, "an' a bloke standin' by the side of the road would think they was a-go'n' to a Sunday-school picnic."

The sergeant was in a talkative mood.

"Lissen to them guns barkin'! We're in for it this time, straight!"

Then, turning to the men behind,--

"'Ave you got yer wills made out, you lads? You're a-go'n' to see a scrap presently, an' it ain't a-go'n' to be no flea-bite, I give you my word!"

"Right you are, sergeant! I'm leavin' me razor to 'is Majesty. 'Ope 'e'll tyke the 'int."

"Strike me pink, sergeant! You gettin' cold feet?"

"Less sing 'im, 'I want to go 'ome.' Get 'im to cryin' like a baby."

"W'ere's yer mouth-organ, Ginger?"

"Right-O! Myke it weepy now! Slow march!"

"I--want to go 'ome!
I--want to go 'ome!
Jack-Johnsons, coal-boxes, and shrapnel, oh, Lor'!
I don't want to go in the trenches no more.
Send me across the sea
W'ere the Allemand can't shoot me.
Oh, my! I don't want to die!
I--want to go 'ome!"

It is one of the most plaintive and yearning of soldiers' songs. Jack-Johnsons and coal-boxes are two greatly dreaded types of high explosive shells which Tommy would much rather sing about than meet.

"Wite," the sergeant said, smiling grimly; "just wite till we reach the end o' this 'ere march! You'll be a-singin' that song out o' the other side o' yer faces."

We halted in the evening at a little mining village, and were billeted for the night in houses, stables, and even in the water-soaked fields, for there was not sufficient accommodation for all of us. With a dozen of my comrades I slept on the floor in the kitchen of a miner's cottage, and listened, far into the night, to the constant procession of motor ambulances, the tramp of marching feet, the thunder of guns, the rattle of windows, and the sound of breaking glass.

The following day we spent in cleaning our rifles, which were caked with rust, and in washing our clothes. We had to put these, still wet, into our packs, for at dusk we fell in, in column of route, along the village street, when our officers told us what was before us. I remember how vividly and honestly one of them described the situation.

"Listen carefully, men. We are moving off in a few moments, to take over captured German trenches on the left of Loos. No one knows yet just how the land lies there. The reports we have had are confused and rather conflicting. The boys you are going to relieve have been having a hard time. The trenches are full of dead. Those who are left are worn out with the strain, and they need sleep. They won't care to stop long after you come in, so you must not expect much information from them. You will have to find out things for yourselves. But I know you well enough to feel certain that you will. From now on you'll not have it easy. You will have to sit tight under a heavy fire from the German batteries. You will have to repulse counter-attacks, for they will make every effort to retake those trenches. But remember! You're British soldiers! Whatever happens you've got to hang on!"

We marched down a road nearly a foot deep in mud. It had been churned to a thick paste by thousands of feet and all the heavy wheel traffic incident to the business of war. The rain was still coming down steadily, and it was pitch dark, except for the reflected light, on the low-hanging clouds, of the flashes from the guns of our batteries and those of the bursting shells of the enemy. We halted frequently, to make way for long files of ambulances which moved as rapidly as the darkness and the awful condition of the roads would permit. I counted twenty of them during one halt, and then stopped, thinking of the pain of the poor fellows inside, their wounds wrenched and torn by the constant pitching and jolting. We had vivid glimpses of them by the light from flashing guns, and of the Red Cross attendants at the rear of the cars, steadying the upper tiers of stretchers on either side. The heavy Garrison artillery was by this time far behind us. The big shells went over with a hollow roar like the sound of an express train heard at a distance. Field artillery was concealed in the ruins of houses on every side. The guns were firing at a tremendous rate, the shells exploding several miles away with a sound of jarring thunder claps.

In addition to the ambulances there was a constant stream of outgoing traffic of other kinds: dispatch riders on motor cycles, feeling their way cautiously along the side of the road; ammunition supply and battalion transport wagons, the horses rearing and plunging in the darkness. We approached a crossroad and halted to make way for some batteries of field pieces moving to new positions. They went by on a slippery cobbled road, the horses at a dead gallop. In the red lightenings of heavy-gun fire they looked like a series of splendid sculptured groups.

We moved on and halted, moved on again, stumbled into ditches to get out of the way of headquarters cars and motor lorries, jumped up and pushed on. Every step through the thick mud was taken with an effort. We frequently lost touch with the troops ahead of us and would have to march at the double in order to catch up. I was fast getting into that despondent, despairing frame of mind which often follows great physical weariness, when I remembered a bit of wisdom out of a book by William James which I had read several years before. He had said, in effect, that men have layers of energy, reserves of nervous force, which they are rarely called upon to use, but which are, nevertheless, assets of great value in times of strain. I had occasion to test the truth of this statement during that night march, and at intervals later, when I felt that I had reached the end of my resources of strength. And I found it to be practical wisdom which stood me in good stead on more than one occasion.

We halted to wait for our trench guides at the village of Vermelles, about three miles back of our lines. The men lay down thankfully in the mud and many were soon asleep despite the terrific noise. Our batteries, concealed in the ruins of houses, were keeping up a steady fire and the German guns were replying almost as hotly. The weird flashes lit up the shattered walls with a fascinating, bizarre effect. By their light, I saw men lying with their heads thrown back over their pack-sacks, their rifles leaning across their bodies; others standing in attitudes of suspended animation. The noise was deafening. One was thrown entirely upon his own resources for comfort and companionship, for it was impossible to converse. While we were waiting for the order to move, a homeless dog put his cold nose into my hand. I patted him and he crept up close beside me. Every muscle in his body was quivering. I wanted to console him in his own language. But I knew very little French, and I should have had to shout into his ear at the top of my voice to have made myself heard. When we marched on I lost him. And I never saw him again.

There was a further march of two and a half miles over open country, the scene of the great battle. The ground was a maze of abandoned trenches and was pitted with shell holes. The clay was so slippery and we were so heavily loaded that we fell down at every step. Some of the boys told me afterward that I cursed like blue blazes all the way up. I was not conscious of this, but I can readily understand that it may have been true. At any rate, as a result of that march, I lost what reputation I had for being temperate in the use of profanity.

We crossed what had been the first line of British trenches, which marked the starting-point of the advance, and from there the ground was covered with the bodies of our comrades, men who had "done their bit," as Tommy says, and would never go home again. Some were huddled in pathetic little groups of two or three as they might have crept together for companionship before they died. Some were lying face downward just as they had fallen. Others in attitudes revealing dreadful suffering. Many were hanging upon the tangles of German barbed wire which the heaviest of bombardments never completely destroys. We saw them only by the light of distant trench rockets and stumbled on them and over them when the darkness returned.

It is an unpleasant experience, marching under fire, on top of the ground, even though it is dark and the enemy is shelling haphazardly. We machine gunners were always heavily loaded. In addition to the usual infantryman's burden, we had our machine guns to carry, and our ammunition, water supply, tools and instruments. We were very eager to get under cover, but we had to go slowly. By the time we reached our trench we were nearly exhausted.

The men whom we were to relieve were packed up, ready to move out, when we arrived. We threw our rifles and equipment on the parapet and stood close to the side of the trench to allow them to pass. They were cased in mud. Their faces, which I saw by the glow of matches or lighted cigarettes, were haggard and worn. A week's growth of beard gave them a wild and barbaric appearance. They talked eagerly. They were hysterically cheerful; voluble from sheer nervous reaction. They had the prospect of getting away for a little while from the sickening horrors: the sight of maimed and shattered bodies, the deafening noise, the nauseating odor of decaying flesh. As they moved out there were the usual conversations which take place between incoming and outgoing troops.

"Wot sort of a week you 'ad, mate?"

"It ain't been a week, son; it's been a lifetime!"

"Lucky fer us you blokes come in just w'en you did. We've about reached the limit."

"'Ow far we got to go fer water?"

"'Bout two miles. Awful journey! Tyke you all night to do it. You got to stop every minute, they's so much traffic along that trench. Go down Stanley Road about five 'unnerd yards, turn off to yer left on Essex Alley, then yer first right. Brings you right out by the 'ouse w'ere the pump is."

"'Ere's a straight tip! Send yer water fatigue down early in the mornin': three o'clock at the latest. They's thousands usin' that well an' she goes dry arter a little w'ile."

"You blokes want any souvenirs, all you got to do is pick 'em up: 'elmets, revolvers, rifles, German di'ries. You wite till mornin'. You'll see plenty."

"Is this the last line o' Fritzie's trenches?"

"Can't tell you, mate. All we know is, we got 'ere some'ow an' we been a-'oldin' on. My Gawd! It's been awful! They calmed down a bit to-night. You blokes is lucky comin' in just w'en you did."

"I ain't got a pal left out o' my section. You'll see some of 'em. We ain't 'ad time to bury 'em."

They were soon gone and we were left in ignorance of the situation. We knew only approximately the direction of the living enemy and the dead spoke to us only in dumb show, telling us unspeakable things about the horrors of modern warfare.

Fortunately for us, the fire of the German batteries, during our first night in captured trenches, was directed chiefly upon positions to our right and left. The shells from our own batteries were exploding far in advance of our sector of trench, and we judged from this that we were holding what had been the enemy's last line, and that the British artillery were shelling the line along which they would dig themselves in anew. We felt more certain of this later in the night when working parties were sent from the battalion to a point twelve hundred yards in front of the trenches we were then holding. They were to dig a new line there, to connect with intrenchments which had been pushed forward on either side of us.

At daybreak we learned that we were slightly to the left of Hill 70. Hulluch, a small village still in possession of the Germans, was to our left front. Midway between Hill 70 and Hulluch and immediately to the front of our position, there was a long stretch of open country which sloped gently forward for six or eight hundred yards, and then rose gradually toward the sky-line. In the first assault the British troops had pushed on past the trenches we were holding and had advanced up the opposite slope, nearly a mile farther on. There they started to dig themselves in, but an unfortunate delay in getting forward had given the enemy time to collect a strong force of local reserves behind his second line, which was several hundred yards beyond. So heavy a fire had been concentrated upon them that the British troops had been forced to retire to the line we were then occupying. They had met with heavy losses both in advancing and retiring, and the ground in front of us for nearly a mile was strewn with bodies. We did not learn all of this at once. We knew nothing of our exact position during the first night, but as there appeared to be no enemy within striking distance of our immediate front, we stood on the firing-benches vainly trying to get our bearings. About one o'clock, we witnessed the fascinating spectacle of a counter-attack at night.

It came with the dramatic suddenness, the striking spectacular display, of a motion-picture battle. The pictorial effect seemed extravagantly overdrawn.

There was a sudden hurricane of rifle and machine-gun fire, and in an instant all the desolate landscape was revealed under the light of innumerable trench rockets. We saw the enemy advancing in irregular lines to the attack. They were exposed to a pitiless infantry fire. I could follow the curve of our trenches on the left by the almost solid sheet of flame issuing from the rifles of our comrades against whom the assault was launched. The artillery ranged upon the advancing lines at once, and the air was filled with the roar of bursting shells and the melancholy whing-g-g-g of flying shrapnel.

I did not believe that any one could cross that fire-swept area alive, but before many moments we heard the staccato of bursting bombs and hand grenades which meant that some of the enemy, at least, were within striking distance. There was a sharp crescendo of deafening sound, then, gradually, the firing ceased, and word came down the line, "Counter-attack against the ---- Guards; and jolly well beaten off too." Another was attempted before daybreak, and again the same torrent of lead, the same hideous uproar, the same sickening smell of lyddite, the same ghastly noon-day effect, the same gradual silence, and the same result.

II. DAMAGED TRENCHES

The brief respite which we enjoyed during our first night soon came to an end. We were given time, however, to make our trenches tenable. Early the following morning we set to work removing the wreckage of human bodies. Never before had death revealed itself so terribly to us. Many of the men had been literally blown to pieces, and it was necessary to gather the fragments in blankets. For weeks afterward we had to eat and sleep and work and think among such awful sights. We became hardened to them finally. It was absolutely essential that we should.

The trenches and dugouts had been battered to pieces by the British artillery fire before the infantry assault, and since their capture the work of destruction had been carried on by the German gunners. Even in their wrecked condition we could see how skillfully they had been constructed. No labor had been spared in making them as nearly shell-proof and as comfortable for living quarters as it is possible for such earthworks to be. The ground here was unusually favorable. Under a clayish surface soil, there was a stratum of solid chalk. Advantage of this had been taken by the German engineers who must have planned and supervised the work. Many of the shell-proof dugouts were fifteen and even twenty feet below the surface of the ground. Entrance to these was made in the front wall of the trench on a level with the floor. Stairways just large enough to permit the passage of a man's body led down to them. The roofs were reinforced with heavy timbers. They were so strongly built throughout that most of them were intact, although the passageways leading up to the trench were choked with loose earth.

There were larger surface dugouts with floors but slightly lower than that of the trench. These were evidently built for living quarters in times of comparative quiet. Many of them were six feet wide and from twenty to thirty feet long, and quite palaces compared to the wretched little "funk-holes" to which we had been accustomed. They were roofed with logs a foot or more in diameter placed close together and one on top of the other in tiers of three, with a covering of earth three or four feet thick. But although they were solidly built they had not been proof against the rain of high explosives. Many of them were in ruins, the logs splintered like kindling wood and strewn far and wide over the ground.

We found several dugouts, evidently officers' quarters, which were almost luxuriously furnished. There were rugs for the wooden floors and pictures and mirrors for the walls; and in each of them there was the jolliest little stove with a removable lid. We discovered one of these underground palaces at the end of a blind alley leading off from the main trench. It was at least fifteen feet underground, with two stairways leading down to it, so that if escape was cut off in one direction, it was still possible to get out on the other side. We immediately took possession, built a roaring fire, and were soon passing canteens of hot tea around the circle. Life was worth while again. We all agreed that there were less comfortable places in which to have breakfast on rainy autumn mornings than German officers' dug-outs.

The haste with which the Germans abandoned their trenches was evidenced by the amount of war material which they left behind. We found two machine guns and a great deal of small-arms ammunition in our own limited sector of frontage. Rifles, intrenching tools, haversacks, canteens, greatcoats, bayonets were scattered everywhere. All of this material was of the very best. Canteens, water-bottles, and small frying-pans were made of aluminum and most ingeniously fashioned to make them less bulky for carrying. Some of the bayonets were saw-edged. We found three of these needlessly cruel weapons in a dugout which bore the following inscription over the door:--

"Gott tret' herein. Bring' glueck herein."

It was an interesting commentary on German character. Tommy Atkins never writes inscriptions of a religious nature over the doorway of his splinter-roof shelter. Neither does he file a saw edge on his bayonet.

We found many letters, picture post-cards, and newspapers; among the latter, one called the "Krieg-Zeitung," published at Lille for the soldiers in the field, and filled with glowing accounts of battles fought by the ever victorious German armies.

Death comes swiftly in war. One's life hangs by a thread. The most trivial circumstance saves or destroys. Mac came into the half-ruined dugout where the off-duty machine gunners were making tea over a fire of splintered logs.

"Jamie," he said, "take my place at sentry for a few minutes, will you? I've lost my water-bottle. It's 'ere in the dugout somew'ere. I'll be only a minute."

I went out to the gun position a few yards away, and immediately afterward the Germans began a bombardment of our line. One's ear becomes exact in distinguishing the size of shells by the sound which they make in traveling through the air; and it is possible to judge the direction and the probable place of their fall. Two of us stood by the machine gun. We heard at the same time the sound which we knew meant danger, possibly death. It was the awful whistling roar of a high explosive. We dropped to the floor of the trench at once. The explosion blackened our faces with lyddite and half-blinded us. The dugout which I had left less than a moment ago was a mass of wreckage. Seven of our comrades were inside.

One of them crawled out, pulling himself along with one arm. The other arm was terribly crushed and one leg was hanging by a tendon and a few shreds of flesh.

"My God, boys! Look wot they did to me!"

He kept saying it over and over while we cut the cords from our bandoliers, tied them about his leg and arm and twisted them up to stop the flow of blood. He was a fine, healthy lad. A moment before he had been telling us what he was going to do when we went home on furlough. Now his face was the color of ashes, his voice grew weaker and weaker, and he died while we were working over him.

High explosive shells were bursting all along the line. Great masses of earth and chalk were blown in on top of men seeking protection where there was none. The ground rocked like so much pasteboard. I heard frantic cries for "Picks and shovels!" "Stretcher-bearers! Stretcher-bearers this way, for God's sake!" The voices sounded as weak and futile as the squeaking of rats in a thunderstorm.

When the bombardment began, all off-duty men were ordered into the deepest of the shell-proof dugouts, where they were really quite safe. But those English lads were not cowards. Orders or no orders, they came out to the rescue of their comrades. They worked without a thought of their own danger. I felt actually happy, for I was witnessing splendid heroic things. It was an experience which gave one a new and unshakable faith in his fellows.

The sergeant and I rushed into the ruins of our machine-gun dugout. The roof still held in one place. There we found Mac, his head split in two as though it had been done with an axe. Gardner's head was blown completely off, and his body was so terribly mangled that we did not know until later who he was. Preston was lying on his back with a great jagged, blood-stained hole through his tunic. Bert Powel was so badly hurt that we exhausted our supply of field dressings in bandaging him. We found little Charlie Harrison lying close to the side of the wall, gazing at his crushed foot with a look of incredulity and horror pitiful to see. One of the men gave him first aid with all the deftness and tenderness of a woman.

The rest of us dug hurriedly into a great heap of earth at the other end of the shelter. We quickly uncovered Walter, a lad who had kept us laughing at his drollery on many a rainy night. The earth had been heaped loosely on him and he was still conscious.

"Good old boys," he said weakly; "I was about done for."

In our haste we dislodged another heap of earth which completely buried him again, and it seemed a lifetime before we were able to remove it. I have never seen a finer display of pure grit than Walter's.

"Easy now!" he said. "Can't feel anything below me waist. I think I'm 'urt down there."

We worked as swiftly and as carefully as we could. We knew that he was badly wounded, for the earth was soaked with blood; but when we saw, we turned away sick with horror. Fortunately, he lost consciousness while we were trying to disentangle him from the fallen timbers, and he died on the way to the field dressing-station. Of the seven lads in the dugout, three were killed outright, three died within half an hour, and one escaped with a crushed foot which had to be amputated at the field hospital.

What had happened to our little group was happening to others along the entire line. Americans may have read of the bombardment which took place that autumn morning. The dispatches, I believe, described it with the usual official brevity, giving all the information really necessary from the point of view of the general public.

"Along the Loos-La Bassee sector there was a lively artillery action. We demolished some earthworks in the vicinity of Hulluch. Some of our trenches near Hill 70 were damaged."

"Damaged!" It was a guarded admission. Our line was a shambles of loose earth and splintered logs. At some places it was difficult to see just where the trench had been. Had the Germans launched a counter-attack immediately after the bombardment, we should have had difficulty in holding the position. But it was only what Tommy called "a big 'ap'orth o' 'ate." No attempt was made to follow up the advantage, and we at once set to work rebuilding. The loose earth had to be put into sandbags, the parapets mended, the holes, blasted out by shells, filled in.

The worst of it was that we could not get away from the sight of the mangled bodies of our comrades. Arms and legs stuck out of the wreckage, and on every side we saw distorted human faces, the faces of men we had known, with whom we had lived and shared hardships and dangers for months past. Those who have never lived through experiences of this sort cannot possibly know the horror of them. It is not in the heat of battle that men lose their reason. Battle frenzy is, perhaps, a temporary madness. The real danger comes when the strain is relaxed. Men look about them and see the bodies of their comrades torn to pieces as though they had been hacked and butchered by fiends. One thinks of the human body as inviolate, a beautiful and sacred thing. The sight of it dismembered or disemboweled, trampled in the bottom of a trench, smeared with blood and filth, is so revolting as to be hardly endurable.

And yet, we had to endure it. We could not escape it. Whichever way we looked, there were the dead. Worse even than the sight of dead men were the groans and entreaties of those lying wounded in the trenches waiting to be taken back to the dressing-stations.

"I'm shot through the stomach, matey! Can't you get me back to the ambulance? Ain't they some way you can get me back out o' this?"

"Stick it, old lad! You won't 'ave long to wite. They'll be some of the Red Cross along 'ere in a jiffy now."

"Give me a lift, boys, can't you? Look at my leg! Do you think it'll 'ave to come off? Maybe they could save it if I could get to 'ospital in time! Won't some of you give me a lift? I can 'obble along with a little 'elp."

"Don't you fret, sonny! You're a-go'n' to ride back in a stretcher presently. Keep yer courage up a little w'ile longer."

Some of the men, in their suffering, forgot every one but themselves, and it was not strange that they should. Others, with more iron in their natures, endured fearful agony in silence. During memorable half-hours, filled with danger and death, many of my gross misjudgments of character were made clear to me. Men whom no one had credited with heroic qualities revealed them. Others failed rather pitiably to live up to one's expectations. It seemed to me that there was strength or weakness in men, quite apart from their real selves, for which they were in no way responsible; but doubtless it had always been there, waiting to be called forth at just such crucial times.

During the afternoon I heard for the first time the hysterical cry of a man whose nerve had given way. He picked up an arm and threw it far out in front of the trenches, shouting as he did so in a way that made one's blood run cold. Then he sat down and started crying and moaning. He was taken back to the rear, one of the saddest of casualties in a war of inconceivable horrors. I heard of many instances of nervous breakdown, but I witnessed surprisingly few of them. Men were often badly shaken and trembled from head to foot. Usually they pulled themselves together under the taunts of their less susceptible comrades.

III. RISSOLES AND A REQUIEM

At the close of a gloomy October day, six unshaven, mud-encrusted machine gunners, the surviving members of two teams, were gathered at the C Company gun emplacement. D Company's gun had been destroyed by a shell, and so we had joined forces here in front of the wrecked dugout, and were waiting for night when we could bury our dead comrades. A fine drenching rain was falling. We sat with our waterproof sheets thrown over our shoulders and our knees drawn up to our chins, that we might conserve the damp warmth of our bodies. No one spoke. No reference was made to our dead comrades who were lying there so close that we could almost touch them from where we sat. Nevertheless, I believe that we were all thinking of them, however unwillingly. I tried to see them as they were only a few hours before. I tried to remember the sound of their voices, how they had laughed; but I could think only of the appearance of their mutilated bodies.

On a dreary autumn evening one's thoughts often take a melancholy turn, even though one is indoors, sitting before a pleasant fire, and hearing but faintly the sighing of the wind and the sound of the rain beating against the window. It is hardly to be wondered at that soldiers in trenches become discouraged at times, and on this occasion, when an unquenchably cheerful voice shouted over an adjoining traverse,--

"Wot che'r, lads! Are we downhearted?"--a growling chorus answered with an unmistakable,--

"YES!"

We were in an open ditch. The rain was beating down on our faces. We were waiting for darkness when we could go to our unpleasant work of grave-digging. To-morrow there would be more dead bodies and more graves to dig, and the day after, the same duty, and the day after that, the same. Week after week we should be living like this, killing and being killed, binding up terrible wounds, digging graves, always doing the same work with not one bright or pleasant thing to look forward to.

These were my thoughts as I sat on the firing-bench with my head drawn down between my knees watching the water dripping from the edges of my puttees. But I had forgotten one important item in the daily routine: supper. And I had forgotten Private Lemley, our cook, or, to give him his due, our chef. He was not the man to waste his time in gloomy reflection. With a dozen mouldy potatoes which he had procured Heaven knows where, four tins of corned beef, and a canteen lid filled with bacon grease for raw materials, he had set to work with the enthusiasm of the born artist, the result being rissoles, brown, crisp, and piping hot. It is a pleasure to think of that meal. Private Lemley was one of the rare souls of earth, one of the Mark Tapleys who never lost his courage or his good spirits. I remember how our spirits rose at the sound of his voice, and how gladly and quickly we responded to his summons.

"'Ere you are, me lads! Bully beef rissoles an' 'ot tea, an' it ain't 'arf bad fer the trenches if I do s'y it."

I can only wonder now at the keenness of our appetites in the midst of the most gruesome surroundings. Dead men were lying about us, both in the trenches and outside of them. And yet our rissoles were not a whit the less enjoyable on that account.

It was quite dark when we had finished. The sergeant jumped to his feet.

"Let's get at it, boys," he said.

Half an hour later we erected a wooden cross in Tommy's grave-strewn garden. It bore the following inscription written in pencil:

>Pte. # 4326 MacDonald.
>Pte. # 7864 Gardner.
>Pte. # 9851 Preston.
>Pte. # 6940 Allen.
> Royal Fusiliers.
> "They did their bit."

Quietly we slipped back into the trench and piled our picks and shovels on the parados.

"Got yer mouth-organ 'andy, Nobby?" some one asked.

"She's always 'andy. Wot'll you 'ave, lads?"

"Give us 'Silk 'At Nat Tony.' That's a proper funeral 'ymn."

"Right you are! Sing up, now!"

And then we sang Tommy's favorite kind of requiem:--

>"I'm Silk Hat Nat Tony,
>I'm down and I'm stony:
>I'm not only broke, but I'm bent.
>The fringe of my trousers
>Keeps lashing the houses,
>But still I am gay and content.

I stroll the West gayly,
You'll see me there daily,
From Burlington Arcade
Up to the Old Bailey.
I'm stony! I'm Tony!
But that makes no diff'rence, you see.
Though I haven't a fraction,
I've this satisfaction,
They built Piccadilly for me."

CHAPTER XI
"SITTING TIGHT"

I. LEMONS AND CRICKET BALLS

Throughout October we fulfilled the prophecy of the officer who told us that "sitting tight" in the German trenches was to be our function. There were nightly counter-attacks preceded by heavy artillery fire, when the enemy made determined efforts to retake the lost territory. There were needless alarms when nervous sentries "got the wind up," to use the authentic trench expression, and contagious excitement set men to firing like mad into blank darkness. In the daytime there were moments of calm which we could not savor owing to that other warfare waged upon us by increasing hordes of parasitic enemies. We moved from one position to another through trenches where the tangled mass of telephone wires, seemingly gifted with a kind of malignant humor, coiled themselves about our feet or caught in the piling swivels of our rifles. There were orders and counter-orders, alarums and excursions. Through them all Tommy kept his balance and his air of cheery unconcern, but he wished that he might be "struck pink" if he knew "wot we was a-doin' of anyw'y."

Our ideas of the tactical situation were decidedly vague. However, we did know, in a general way, our position with reference to important military landmarks, and the amateur strategists were busy at all times explaining the situation to frankly ignorant comrades, and outlining plans for definite action.

"Now, if I was General French, I'd make 'Ulluch me main objective. They ain't no use tryin' to get by at this part o' the line till you got that village."

"Don't talk so bloomin' ignorant! Ain't that just wot they been a-tryin'? Wot we got to do is go 'round 'Ulluch. Tyke 'em in the rear an' from both sides."

"W'y don't they get on with it? Wot to blazes are we a-doin' of, givin' 'em a chanct to get dug in again? 'Ere we all but got 'em on the run an' the 'ole show stops!"

The continuation of the offensive was the chief topic of conversation. The men dreaded it, but they were anxious to get through with the business. They believed that now if ever there was the chance to push the Germans out of France.

In the mean time the day's work was still the day's work. There were nightly bombing affairs, some of them most desperate hand-to-hand contests for the possession of small sectors of trench. One of these I witnessed from a trench sixty yards away. The advantage lay with us. The enemy held only the center of the line and were forced to meet attacks from either end. However, they had a communication trench connecting with their second line, through which carrying parties brought them a limitless supply of bombs.

The game of pitch and toss over the barricades had continued for several days without a decision. Then came orders for more decisive action. The barricades were to be destroyed and the enemy bombed out. In underground fighting of this kind the element of surprise is possible. If one opponent can be suddenly overwhelmed with a heavy rain of bombs, the chances of success for the attacking party are quite favorable.

The action took place at dusk. Shortly before the hour set, the bombers, all of them boys in their early twenties, filed slowly along the trench, the pockets of their grenade waistcoats bulging with "lemons" and "cricket balls," as the two most effective kinds of bombs are called. They went to their places with that spirit of stolid cheeriness which is the wonder and admiration of every one who knows Tommy Atkins intimately. Formerly, when I saw him in this mood, I would think, "He doesn't realize. Men don't go out to meet death like this." But long association with him had convinced me of the error of this opinion. These men knew that death or terrible injury was in store for many of them; yet they were talking in excited and gleeful undertones, as they might have passed through the gates at a football match.

"Are we downhearted? Not likely, old son!"

"Tyke a feel o' this little puffball! Smack on old Fritzie's napper she goes!"

"I'm a-go'n' to arsk fer a nice Blightey one! Four months in Brentford 'ospital an' me Christmas puddin' at 'ome!"

"Now, don't ferget, you blokes! County o' London War 'Ospital fer me if I gets a knock! Write it on a piece o' pyper an' pin it to me tunic w'en you sends me back to the ambulance."

The barricades were blown up and the fight was on. A two-hundred-piece orchestra of blacksmiths, with sledgehammers, beating kettle-drums the size of brewery vats, might have approximated, in quality and volume, the sound of the battle. The spectacular effect was quite different from that of a counter-attack across the open. Lurid flashes of light issued from the ground as though a door to the infernal regions had been thrown jarringly open. The cloud of thick smoke was shot through with red gleams. Men ran along the parapet hurling bombs down into the trench. Now they were hidden by the smoke, now silhouetted for an instant against a glare of blinding light.

An hour passed and there was no change in the situation.

"Fritzie's a tough old bird," said Tommy. "'E's a-go'n' to die game, you got to give it to 'im."

The excitement was intense. Urgent calls for "More lemons! More cricket balls!" were sent back constantly. Box after box, each containing a dozen grenades, was passed up the line from hand to hand, and still the call for "More bombs!" We couldn't send them up fast enough.

The wounded were coming back in twos and threes. One lad, his eyes covered with a bloody bandage, was led by another with a shattered hand.

"Poor old Tich! She went off right in 'is face! But you did yer bit, Tich! You ought to 'a' seen 'im, you blokes! Wasn't 'e a-lettin' 'em 'ave it!"

Another man hobbled past on one foot, supporting himself against the side of the trench.

"Got a Blightey one," he said gleefully. "So long you lads! I'll be with you again arter the 'olidays."

Those who do not know the horrors of modern warfare cannot readily understand the joy of the soldier at receiving a wound which is not likely to prove serious. A bullet in the arm or the shoulder, even though it shatters the bone, or a piece of shrapnel or shell casing in the leg, was always a matter for congratulation.

These were "Blightey wounds." When Tommy received one of this kind, he was a candidate for hospital in "Blightey," as England is affectionately called. For several months he would be far away from the awful turmoil. His body would be clean; he would be rid of the vermin and sleep comfortably in a bed at night. The strain would be relaxed, and, who knows, the war might be over before he was again fit for active service. And so the less seriously wounded made their way painfully but cheerfully along the trench, on their way to the field dressing-station, the motor ambulance, the hospital ship, and--home! while their unwounded comrades gave them words of encouragement and good cheer.

"Good luck to you, Sammy boy! If you sees my missus, tell 'er I'm as right as rain!"

"Sammy, you lucky blighter! W'en yer convalescin', 'ave a pint of ale at the W'ite Lion fer me."

"An' a good feed o' fish an' chips fer me, Sammy. Mind yer foot! There's a 'ole just 'ere!"

"'Ere comes old Sid! W'ere you caught it, mate?"

"In me bloomin' shoulder. It ain't 'arf givin' it to me!"

"Never you mind, Sid! Blightey fer you, boy!"

"Hi, Sid! Tell me old lady I'm still up an' comin', will you? You know w'ere she lives, forty-six Bromley Road."

One lad, his nerve gone, pushed his way frantically down the trench. He had "funked it." He was hysterical with fright and crying in a dry, shaking voice,--

"It's too 'orrible! I can't stand it! Blow you to 'ell they do! Look at me! I'm slathered in blood! I can't stand it! They ain't no man can stand it!"

He met with scant courtesy. A trench during an attack is no place for the fainthearted. An unsympathetic Tommy kicked him savagely.

"Go 'ide yerself, you bloody little coward!"

"More lemons! More cricket balls!" and at last, Victory! Fritzie had "chucked it," and men of the Royal Engineers, that wonderfully efficient corps, were on the spot with picks and shovels and sandbags, clearing out the wreckage, and building a new barricade at the farther end of the communication trench.

It was only a minor affair, one of many which take place nightly in the firingline. Twoscore yards of trench were captured. The cost was, perhaps, one man per yard; but as Tommy said,--

"It ain't the trench wot counts. It's the more-ale. Bucks the blokes up to win, an' that's worth a 'ole bloomin' army corps."

II. "GO IT, THE NORFOLKS!"

Rumors of all degrees of absurdity reached us. The enemy was massing on our right, on our left, on our immediate front. The division was to attack at dawn under cover of a hundred bomb-dropping battle-planes. Units of the new armies to the number of five hundred thousand were concentrating behind the line from La Bassee to Arras, and another tremendous drive was to be made in conjunction with the French, (As a matter of fact, we knew less of what was actually happening than did people in England and America.) Most of these reports sprang, full grown, from the fertile brains of officers' servants. Scraps of information which they gathered while in attendance at the officers' mess dugout were pieced together, and much new material of their own invention added. The striving was for piquancy rather than plausibility. A wild tale was always better than a dull one; furthermore the "batmen" were our only sources of official information, and could always command a hearing. When one of them came down the trench with that mysterious "I-could-a-tale-unfold" air, he was certain to be halted by willingly gullible comrades.

"Wot's up, Jerry? Anything new?"

"Nor 'arf! Now, keep this under yer 'ats, you blokes! My gov'nor was a-talkin' to Major Bradley this mornin' w'ile I was a-mykin' 'is tea, an' ' e says--"

Then followed the thrilling narrative, a disclosure of official secrets while groups of war-worn Tommies listened with eager interest. "Spreading the News" was a tragi-comedy enacted daily in the trenches.

But we were not entirely in the dark. The signs which preceded an engagement were unmistakable, and toward the middle of October there was general agreement that an important action was about to take place. British aircraft had been patrolling our front ceaselessly for hours. Several battalions (including our own which had just gone into reserve at Vermelles) were placed on bomb-carrying fatigue. As we went up to the firing-line with our first load, we found all of the support trenches filled to overflowing with troops in fighting order.

We reached the first line as the preliminary bombardment started. Scores of batteries were concentrating their fire on the enemy's trenches directly opposite us. It is useless to attempt to depict what lay before us as we looked over the parapet. The trenches were hidden from view in a cloud of smoke and flame and dirt. The earth was like a muddy sea dashed high in spray against hidden rocks.

The men who were to lead the attack were standing rifle in hand, waiting for the sudden cessation of fire which would be the signal for them to mount the parapet. Bombers and bayonet-men alternated in series of two. The bombers wore their mediaeval-looking shrapnel-proof helmets and heavy canvas grenade coats with twelve pockets sagging with bombs. Their rifles were slung on their backs to give them free use of their hands.

Every one was smoking--some calmly, some with short, nervous puffs. It was interesting to watch the faces of the men. One could read, almost to a certainty, what was going on in their minds. Some of them were thinking of the terrible events so near at hand. They were imagining the horrors of the attack in detail. Others were unconcernedly intent upon adjusting straps of their equipment, or in rubbing their clips of ammunition with an oily rag. Several men were singing to a mouth-organ accompaniment. I saw their lips moving, but not a sound reached me above the din of the guns, although I was standing only a few yards distant. It was like an absurd pantomime.

As I watched them, the sense of the unreality of the whole thing swept over me more strongly than ever before. "This can't be true," I thought; "I have never been a soldier. There isn't any European war." I had the curious feeling that my body and brain were functioning quite apart from me. I was only a slow-witted, incredulous spectator looking on with a stupid animal wonder. I have learned that this feeling is quite common among men in the trenches. A part of the mind works normally, and another part, which seems to be one's essential self, refuses to assimilate and classify experiences so unusual, so different from anything in the catalogue of memory.

For two hours and a half the roar of guns continued. Then it stopped as suddenly as it had begun. An officer near me shouted, "Now, men! Follow me!" and clambered over the parapet. There was no hesitation. In a moment the trench was empty save for the bomb-carrying parties and an artillery observation officer, who was jumping up and down on the firing-bench, shouting--

"Go it, the Norfolks! Go it, the Norfolks! My God! Isn't it fine! Isn't it splendid!"

There you have the British officer true to type. He is a sportsman: next to taking part in a fight he loves to see one--and he says "isn't" not "ain't," even under stress of the greatest excitement.

The German artillery, which had been reserving fire, now poured forth a deluge of shrapnel. The sound of rifle fire was scattered and ragged at first, but it increased steadily in volume. Then came the "boiler-factory chorus," the sharp rattle of dozens of machine guns. The bullets were flying over our heads like swarms of angry wasps. A ration-box board which I held above the parapet was struck almost immediately. Fortunately for the artillery officer, a disrespectful N.C.O. pulled him down into the trench.

"It's no use throwin' yer life aw'y, sir. You won't 'elp 'em over by barkin' at 'em."

He was up again almost at once, coolly watching the progress of the troops from behind a small barricade of sandbags, and reporting upon it to batteries several miles in rear. The temptation to look over the parapet was not to be resisted. The artillery lengthened their ranges. I saw the curtain of flame-shot smoke leap at a bound to the next line of German trenches.

Within a few moments several lines of reserves filed into the front trench and went over the parapet in support of the first line, advancing with heads down like men bucking into the fury of a gale. We saw them only for an instant as they jumped to their feet outside the trench and rushed forward. Many were hit before they had passed through the gaps in our barbed wire. Those who were able crept back and were helped into the trench by comrades. One man was killed as he was about to reach a place of safety. He lay on the parapet with his head and arms hanging down inside the trench. His face was that of a boy of twenty-one or twenty-two. I carry the memory of it with me to-day as vividly as when I left the trenches in November.

Following the attacking infantry were those other soldiers whose work, though less spectacular than that of the riflemen, was just as essential and quite as dangerous. Royal Engineers, with picks and shovels and sandbags, rushed forward to reverse the parapets of the captured trenches, and to clear out the wreckage, while the riflemen waited for the launching of the first counter-attack. They were preceded by men of the Signaling Corps, who advanced swiftly and skillfully, unwinding spools of insulated telephone wire as they went. Bomb-carriers, stretcher-bearers, intent upon their widely divergent duties, followed. The work of salvage and destruction went hand in hand.

The battle continued until evening, when we received orders to move up to the firing-line. We started at five o'clock, and although we had less than three miles to go, we did not reach the end of our journey until four the next morning, owing to the fatigue parties and the long stream of wounded which blocked the communication trenches. For more than an hour we lay just outside of the trench looking down on a seemingly endless procession of casualties. Some of the men were crying like children, some groaning pitifully, some laughing despite their wounds. I heard dialects peculiar to every part of England, and fragmentary accounts of hairbreadth escapes and desperate fighting.

"They was a big Dutchman comin' at me from the other side. Lucky fer me that I 'ad a round in me breach. He'd 'a' got me if it 'adn't 'a' been fer that ca'tridge. I let 'im 'ave it an' 'e crumpled up like a wet blanket."

"Seeven of them, an' that dazed like, they wasna good for onything. Mon, it would ha' been fair murder to kill 'em! They wasna wantin' to fight."

Boys scarcely out of their 'teens talked with the air of old veterans. Many of them had been given their first taste of real fighting, and they were experiencing a very common and natural reaction. Their courage had been put to the most severe test and had not given way. It was not difficult to understand their elation, and one could forgive their boastful talk of bloody deeds. One highly strung lad was dangerously near to nervous breakdown. He had bayoneted his first German and could not forget the experience. He told of it over and over as the line moved slowly along.

"I couldn't get me bayonet out," he said. "Wen 'e fell 'e pulled me over on top of 'im. I 'ad to put me foot against 'im an' pull, an' then it came out with a jerk."

We met small groups of prisoners under escort of proud and happy Tommies who gave us conflicting reports of the success of the attack. Some of them said that two more lines of German trenches had been taken; others declared that we had broken completely through and that the enemy were in full retreat. Upon arriving at our position, we were convinced that at least one trench had been captured; but when we mounted our guns and peered cautiously over the parapet, the lights which we saw in the distance were the flashes of German rifles, not the street lamps of Berlin.

III. CHRISTIAN PRACTICE

Meanwhile, the inhumanity of a war without truces was being revealed to us on every hand. Hundreds of bodies were lying between the opposing lines of trenches and there was no chance to bury them. Fatigue parties were sent out at night to dispose of those which were lying close to the parapets, but the work was constantly delayed and interrupted by persistent sniping and heavy shell fire. Others farther out lay where they had fallen day after day and week after week. Many an anxious mother in England was seeking news of a son whose body had become a part of that Flemish landscape.

During the week following the commencement of the offensive, the wounded were brought back in twos and threes from the contested area over which attacks and counter-attacks were taking place. One plucky Englishman was discovered about fifty yards in front of our trenches. He was waving a handkerchief tied to the handle of his intrenching tool. Stretcher-bearers ran out under fire and brought him in. He had been wounded in the foot when his company were advancing up the slope fifteen hundred yards away. When it was found necessary to retire, he had been left with many dead and wounded comrades, far from the possibility of help by friends. He had bandaged his wound with his first-aid field dressing, and started crawling back, a few yards at a time. He secured food from the haversacks of dead comrades, and at length, after a week of painful creeping, reached our lines.

Another of our comrades was discovered by a listening patrol, six days after he had been wounded. He, too, had been struck down close to the enemy's second line. Two kind-hearted German sentries, to whom he had signaled, crept out at night and gave him hot coffee to drink. He begged them to carry him in, but they told him they were forbidden to take any wounded prisoners. As he was unable to crawl, he must have died had it not been for the keen ears of the men of the listening patrol.

A third victim whom I saw was brought in at daybreak by a working party. He had been shot in the jaw and lay unattended through at least five wet October days and nights. His eyes were swollen shut. Blood-poisoning had set in from a wound which would certainly not have been fatal could it have received early attention.

We knew that there must be many wounded still alive in the tall grass between our lines. We knew that many were dying who might be saved. The Red Cross Corps made nightly searches for them, but the difficulties to be overcome were great. The volume of fire increased tremendously at night. Furthermore, there was a wide area to be searched, and in the darkness men lying unconscious, or too weak from the loss of blood to groan or shout, were discovered only by accident.

Tommy Atkins isn't an advocate of "peace at any price," but the sight of awful and needless suffering invariably moved him to declare himself emphatically against the inhuman practices in war of so-called Christian nations.

"Christian nations!" he would say scornfully. "If this 'ere is a sample o' Christianity, I'll tyke me charnces down below w'en I gets knocked out." His comrades greeted such outbursts with hearty approval.

"I'm with you there, mate! 'Ell won't be such a dusty old place if all the Christians go upstairs."

"They ain't no God 'avin' anything to do with this war, I'm telling you! All the religious blokes in England an' France an' Germany ain't a-go'n' to pray 'Im into it!"

I am not in a position to speak for Hans and Fritz, who faced us from the other side of No-Man's-Land; but as for Tommy, it seemed to me that he had a higher opinion of the Deity than many of his better-educated countrymen at home.

IV. TOMMY

By the end of the month we had seen more of suffering and death than it is good for men to see in a lifetime. There were attacks and counter-attacks, hand-to-hand fights in communication trenches with bombs and bayonets, heavy bombardments, nightly burial parties. Tommy Atkins looked like a beast. His clothing was a hardened-mud casing; his body was the color of the sticky Flanders clay in which he lived; but his soul was clean and fine. I saw him rescuing wounded comrades, tending them in the trenches, encouraging them and heartening them when he himself was discouraged and sick at heart.

"You're a-go'n' 'ome, 'Arry! Blimy! think o' that! Back to old Blightey w'ile the rest of us 'as got to stick it out 'ere! Don't I wish I was you! Not 'arf!"

"You ain't bad 'urt! Strike me pink! You'll be as keen as a w'istle in a couple o' months. An' 'ere! Christmas in Blightey, son! S'y! I'll tyke yer busted shoulder if you'll give me the chanct!"

"They ain't nothin' they can't do fer you back at the base 'ospital. 'Member 'ow they fixed old Ginger up? You ain't caught it 'arf as bad!"

In England, before I knew him for the man he is, I said, "How am I to endure living with him?" And now I am thinking, how am I to endure living without him; without the inspiration of his splendid courage; without the visible example of his unselfish devotion to his fellows? There were a few cowards and shirkers who failed to live up to the standard set by their comrades. I remember the man of thirty-five or forty who lay whimpering in the trench when there was unpleasant work to be done, while boys half his age kicked him in a vain attempt to waken him to a sense of duty; but instances of this kind were rare. There were not enough of them to serve as a foil to the shining deeds which were of daily and hourly occurrence.

Tommy is sick of the war--dead sick of it. He is weary of the interminable procession of comfortless nights and days. He is weary of the sight of maimed and bleeding men--of the awful suspense of waiting for death. In the words of his pathetic little song, he does "want to go 'ome." But there is that within him which says, "Hold on!" He is a compound of cheery optimism and grim tenacity which makes him an incomparable fighting man.

The intimate picture of him which lingers most willingly in my mind is that which I carried with me from the trenches on the dreary November evening shortly before I bade him good-bye. It had been raining and sleeting for a week. The trenches were knee-deep in water, in some places waist-deep, for the ground was as level as a floor and there was no possibility of drainage. We were wet through and our legs were numb with the cold. Near our gun position there was a hole in the floor of the trench where the water had collected in a deep pool. A bridge of boards had been built around one side of this, but in the darkness a passer-by slipped and fell into the icy water nearly up to his arm-pits.

"Now, then, matey!" said an exasperating voice, "bathin' in our private pool without a permit?"

And another, "'Ere, son! This ain't a swimmin' bawth! That's our tea water yer a-standin' in!"

The Tommy in the pool must have been nearly frozen, but for a moment he made no attempt to get out.

"One o' you fetch me a bit o' soap, will you?" he said coaxingly. "You ain't a-go'n' to talk about tea water to a bloke wot ain't 'ad a bawth in seven weeks?"

It is men of this stamp who have the fortunes of England in their keeping. And they are called, "The Boys of the Bulldog Breed."

www.bookjungle.com *email: sales@bookjungle.com fax: 630-214-0564 mail: Book Jungle PO Box 2226 Champaign, IL 61825*

The Codes Of Hammurabi And Moses
W. W. Davies

QTY

The discovery of the Hammurabi Code is one of the greatest achievements of archaeology, and is of paramount interest, not only to the student of the Bible, but also to all those interested in ancient history...

Religion   ISBN: *1-59462-338-4*   Pages:132
MSRP $12.95

The Theory of Moral Sentiments
Adam Smith

QTY

This work from 1749. contains original theories of conscience amd moral judgment and it is the foundation for systemof morals.

Philosophy   ISBN: *1-59462-777-0*   Pages:536
MSRP $19.95

Jessica's First Prayer
Hesba Stretton

QTY

In a screened and secluded corner of one of the many railway-bridges which span the streets of London there could be seen a few years ago, from five o'clock every morning until half past eight, a tidily set-out coffee-stall, consisting of a trestle and board, upon which stood two large tin cans, with a small fire of charcoal burning under each so as to keep the coffee boiling during the early hours of the morning when the work-people were thronging into the city on their way to their daily toil...

Pages:84

Childrens   ISBN: *1-59462-373-2*   *MSRP $9.95*

My Life and Work
Henry Ford

QTY

Henry Ford revolutionized the world with his implementation of mass production for the Model T automobile. Gain valuable business insight into his life and work with his own auto-biography... "We have only started on our development of our country we have not as yet, with all our talk of wonderful progress, done more than scratch the surface. The progress has been wonderful enough but..."

Pages:300

Biographies/   ISBN: *1-59462-198-5*   *MSRP $21.95*

www.bookjungle.com *email: sales@bookjungle.com fax: 630-214-0564 mail: Book Jungle PO Box 2226 Champaign, IL 61825*

The Art of Cross-Examination
Francis Wellman

QTY

I presume it is the experience of every author, after his first book is published upon an important subject, to be almost overwhelmed with a wealth of ideas and illustrations which could readily have been included in his book, and which to his own mind, at least, seem to make a second edition inevitable. Such certainly was the case with me; and when the first edition had reached its sixth impression in five months, I rejoiced to learn that it seemed to my publishers that the book had met with a sufficiently favorable reception to justify a second and considerably enlarged edition. ..

Reference   ISBN: *1-59462-647-2*   Pages:412 MSRP *$19.95*

On the Duty of Civil Disobedience
Henry David Thoreau

QTY

Thoreau wrote his famous essay, On the Duty of Civil Disobedience, as a protest against an unjust but popular war and the immoral but popular institution of slave-owning. He did more than write—he declined to pay his taxes, and was hauled off to gaol in consequence. Who can say how much this refusal of his hastened the end of the war and of slavery ?

Law   ISBN: *1-59462-747-9*   Pages:48 MSRP *$7.45*

Dream Psychology Psychoanalysis for Beginners
Sigmund Freud

QTY

Sigmund Freud, born Sigismund Schlomo Freud (May 6, 1856 - September 23, 1939), was a Jewish-Austrian neurologist and psychiatrist who co-founded the psychoanalytic school of psychology. Freud is best known for his theories of the unconscious mind, especially involving the mechanism of repression; his redefinition of sexual desire as mobile and directed towards a wide variety of objects; and his therapeutic techniques, especially his understanding of transference in the therapeutic relationship and the presumed value of dreams as sources of insight into unconscious desires.

Psychology   ISBN: *1-59462-905-6*   Pages:196 MSRP *$15.45*

The Miracle of Right Thought
Orison Swett Marden

QTY

Believe with all of your heart that you will do what you were made to do. When the mind has once formed the habit of holding cheerful, happy, prosperous pictures, it will not be easy to form the opposite habit. It does not matter how improbable or how far away this realization may see, or how dark the prospects may be, if we visualize them as best we can, as vividly as possible, hold tenaciously to them and vigorously struggle to attain them, they will gradually become actualized, realized in the life. But a desire, a longing without endeavor, a yearning abandoned or held indifferently will vanish without realization.

Self Help   ISBN: *1-59462-644-8*   Pages:360 MSRP *$25.45*

www.bookjungle.com email: sales@bookjungle.com fax: 630-214-0564 mail: Book Jungle PO Box 2226 Champaign, IL 61825

QTY

	Title	ISBN	Price
☐	**The Rosicrucian Cosmo-Conception Mystic Christianity** by *Max Heindel*	ISBN: *1-59462-188-8*	**$38.95**

The Rosicrucian Cosmo-conception is not dogmatic, neither does it appeal to any other authority than the reason of the student. It is: not controversial, but is: sent forth in the, hope that it may help to clear... *New Age/Religion Pages 646*

☐ **Abandonment To Divine Providence** by *Jean-Pierre de Caussade* ISBN: *1-59462-228-0* **$25.95**
"The Rev. Jean Pierre de Caussade was one of the most remarkable spiritual writers of the Society of Jesus in France in the 18th Century. His death took place at Toulouse in 1751. His works have gone through many editions and have been republished... *Inspirational/Religion Pages 400*

☐ **Mental Chemistry** by *Charles Haanel* ISBN: *1-59462-192-6* **$23.95**
Mental Chemistry allows the change of material conditions by combining and appropriately utilizing the power of the mind. Much like applied chemistry creates something new and unique out of careful combinations of chemicals the mastery of mental chemistry... *New Age Pages 354*

☐ **The Letters of Robert Browning and Elizabeth Barret Barrett 1845-1846 vol II** ISBN: *1-59462-193-4* **$35.95**
by *Robert Browning* and *Elizabeth Barrett*
Biographies Pages 596

☐ **Gleanings In Genesis (volume I)** by *Arthur W. Pink* ISBN: *1-59462-130-6* **$27.45**
Appropriately has Genesis been termed "the seed plot of the Bible" for in it we have, in germ form, almost all of the great doctrines which are afterwards fully developed in the books of Scripture which follow... *Religion/Inspirational Pages 420*

☐ **The Master Key** by *L. W. de Laurence* ISBN: *1-59462-001-6* **$30.95**
In no branch of human knowledge has there been a more lively increase of the spirit of research during the past few years than in the study of Psychology, Concentration and Mental Discipline. The requests for authentic lessons in Thought Control, Mental Discipline and... *New Age/Business Pages 422*

☐ **The Lesser Key Of Solomon Goetia** by *L. W. de Laurence* ISBN: *1-59462-092-X* **$9.95**
This translation of the first book of the "Lernegton" which is now for the first time made accessible to students of Talismanic Magic was done, after careful collation and edition, from numerous Ancient Manuscripts in Hebrew, Latin, and French... *New Age/Occult Pages 92*

☐ **Rubaiyat Of Omar Khayyam** by *Edward Fitzgerald* ISBN:*1-59462-332-5* **$13.95**
Edward Fitzgerald, whom the world has already learned, in spite of his own efforts to remain within the shadow of anonymity, to look upon as one of the rarest poets of the century, was born at Bredfield, in Suffolk, on the 31st of March, 1809. He was the third son of John Purcell... *Music Pages 172*

☐ **Ancient Law** by *Henry Maine* ISBN: *1-59462-128-4* **$29.95**
The chief object of the following pages is to indicate some of the earliest ideas of mankind, as they are reflected in Ancient Law, and to point out the relation of those ideas to modern thought. *Religiom/History Pages 452*

☐ **Far-Away Stories** by *William J. Locke* ISBN: *1-59462-129-2* **$19.45**
"Good wine needs no bush, but a collection of mixed vintages does. And this book is just such a collection. Some of the stories I do not want to remain buried for ever in the museum files of dead magazine-numbers an author's not unpardonable vanity..." *Fiction Pages 272*

☐ **Life of David Crockett** by *David Crockett* ISBN: *1-59462-250-7* **$27.45**
"Colonel David Crockett was one of the most remarkable men of the times in which he lived. Born in humble life, but gifted with a strong will, an indomitable courage, and unremitting perseverance... *Biographies/New Age Pages 424*

☐ **Lip-Reading** by *Edward Nitchie* ISBN: *1-59462-206-X* **$25.95**
Edward B. Nitchie, founder of the New York School for the Hard of Hearing, now the Nitchie School of Lip-Reading, Inc, wrote "LIP-READING Principles and Practice". The development and perfecting of this meritorious work on lip-reading was an undertaking... *How-to Pages 400*

☐ **A Handbook of Suggestive Therapeutics, Applied Hypnotism, Psychic Science** ISBN: *1-59462-214-0* **$24.95**
by *Henry Munro*
Health/New Age/Health/Self-help Pages 376

☐ **A Doll's House: and Two Other Plays** by *Henrik Ibsen* ISBN: *1-59462-112-8* **$19.95**
Henrik Ibsen created this classic when in revolutionary 1848 Rome. Introducing some striking concepts in playwriting for the realist genre, this play has been studied the world over. *Fiction/Classics/Plays 308*

☐ **The Light of Asia** by *sir Edwin Arnold* ISBN: *1-59462-204-3* **$13.95**
In this poetic masterpiece, Edwin Arnold describes the life and teachings of Buddha. The man who was to become known as Buddha to the world was born as Prince Gautama of India but he rejected the worldly riches and abandoned the reigns of power when... *Religion/History/Biographies Pages 170*

☐ **The Complete Works of Guy de Maupassant** by *Guy de Maupassant* ISBN: *1-59462-157-8* **$16.95**
"For days and days, nights and nights, I had dreamed of that first kiss which was to consecrate our engagement, and I knew not on what spot I should put my lips..." *Fiction/Classics Pages 240*

☐ **The Art of Cross-Examination** by *Francis L. Wellman* ISBN: *1-59462-309-0* **$26.95**
Written by a renowned trial lawyer, Wellman imparts his experience and uses case studies to explain how to use psychology to extract desired information through questioning. *How-to/Science/Reference Pages 408*

☐ **Answered or Unanswered?** by *Louisa Vaughan* ISBN: *1-59462-248-5* **$10.95**
Miracles of Faith in China
Religion Pages 112

☐ **The Edinburgh Lectures on Mental Science (1909)** by *Thomas* ISBN: *1-59462-008-3* **$11.95**
This book contains the substance of a course of lectures recently given by the writer in the Queen Street Hall, Edinburgh. Its purpose is to indicate the Natural Principles governing the relation between Mental Action and Material Conditions... *New Age/Psychology Pages 148*

☐ **Ayesha** by *H. Rider Haggard* ISBN: *1-59462-301-5* **$24.95**
Verily and indeed it is the unexpected that happens! Probably if there was one person upon the earth from whom the Editor of this, and of a certain previous history, did not expect to hear again... *Classics Pages 380*

☐ **Ayala's Angel** by *Anthony Trollope* ISBN: *1-59462-352-X* **$29.95**
The two girls were both pretty, but Lucy who was twenty-one who supposed to be simple and comparatively unattractive, whereas Ayala was credited, as her Bombwhat romantic name might show, with poetic charm and a taste for romance. Ayala when her father died was nineteen... *Fiction Pages 484*

☐ **The American Commonwealth** by *James Bryce* ISBN: *1-59462-286-8* **$34.45**
An interpretation of American democratic political theory. It examines political mechanics and society from the perspective of Scotsman James Bryce *Politics Pages 572*

☐ **Stories of the Pilgrims** by *Margaret P. Pumphrey* ISBN: *1-59462-116-0* **$17.95**
This book explores pilgrims religious oppression in England as well as their escape to Holland and eventual crossing to America on the Mayflower, and their early days in New England... *History Pages 268*

www.bookjungle.com email: sales@bookjungle.com fax: 630-214-0564 mail: Book Jungle PO Box 2226 Champaign, IL 61825

			QTY
The Fasting Cure by *Sinclair Upton*	ISBN: *1-59462-222-1*	**$13.95**	☐

In the Cosmopolitan Magazine for May, 1910, and in the Contemporary Review (London) for April, 1910, I published an article dealing with my experiences in fasting. I have written a great many magazine articles, but never one which attracted so much attention... *New Age/Self Help/Health Pages 164*

Hebrew Astrology by *Sepharial*	ISBN: *1-59462-308-2*	**$13.45**	☐

In these days of advanced thinking it is a matter of common observation that we have left many of the old landmarks behind and that we are now pressing forward to greater heights and to a wider horizon than that which represented the mind-content of our progenitors... *Astrology Pages 144*

Thought Vibration or The Law of Attraction in the Thought World	ISBN: *1-59462-127-6*	**$12.95**	☐
by *William Walker Atkinson*		*Psychology/Religion Pages 144*	

Optimism by *Helen Keller*	ISBN: *1-59462-108-X*	**$15.95**	☐

Helen Keller was blind, deaf, and mute since 19 months old, yet famously learned how to overcome these handicaps, communicate with the world, and spread her lectures promoting optimism. An inspiring read for everyone... *Biographies/Inspirational Pages 84*

Sara Crewe by *Frances Burnett*	ISBN: *1-59462-360-0*	**$9.45**	☐

In the first place, Miss Minchin lived in London. Her home was a large, dull, tall one, in a large, dull square, where all the houses were alike, and all the sparrows were alike, and where all the door-knockers made the same heavy sound... *Childrens/Classic Pages 88*

The Autobiography of Benjamin Franklin by *Benjamin Franklin*	ISBN: *1-59462-135-7*	**$24.95**	☐

The Autobiography of Benjamin Franklin has probably been more extensively read than any other American historical work, and no other book of its kind has had such ups and downs of fortune. Franklin lived for many years in England, where he was agent... *Biographies/History Pages 332*

Name	
Email	
Telephone	
Address	
City, State ZIP	

☐ Credit Card   ☐ Check / Money Order

Credit Card Number	
Expiration Date	
Signature	

Please Mail to: Book Jungle
                  PO Box 2226
                  Champaign, IL 61825
or Fax to: 630-214-0564

ORDERING INFORMATION

web: www.bookjungle.com
email: sales@bookjungle.com
fax: 630-214-0564
mail: Book Jungle PO Box 2226 Champaign, IL 61825
or PayPal to sales@bookjungle.com

Please contact us for bulk discounts

DIRECT-ORDER TERMS

20% Discount if You Order Two or More Books
Free Domestic Shipping!
Accepted: Master Card, Visa, Discover, American Express

www.ingramcontent.com/pod-product-compliance
Lightning Source LLC
Chambersburg PA
CBHW080520110426
42742CB00017B/3181